BUSINESS BASICS

MANAGING MEETINGS

How to prepare, how to take part
and how to follow up effectively

Ann Dobson

How To Books

Cartoons by Mike Flanagan

British Library cataloguing-in-publication data
A catalogue record for this book is available from the British Library.

© Copyright 1996 by Ann Dobson.

Published by How To Books Ltd, Plymbridge House,
Estover Road, Plymouth PL6 7PZ, United Kingdom.

First edition 1996

Note: The material contained in this book is set out in good faith for
general guidance and no liability can be accepted for loss or expense
incurred as a result of relying in particular circumstances on statements
made in the book. The laws and regulations are complex and liable to
change, and readers should check the current position with the relevant
authorities before making personal arrangements.

Produced for How To Books by Deer Park Productions.
Typeset by PDQ Typesetting, Stoke-on-Trent, Staffs.
Printed and bound by The Cromwell Press Ltd, Broughton Gifford,
Melksham, Wiltshire.

MANAGING MEETINGS

Other How To Books on business and management

Be a Freelance Sales Agent
Buy & Run a Shop
Buy & Run a Small Hotel
Communicate at Work
Conduct Staff Appraisals
Conducting Interviews
Doing Business Abroad
Do Your Own Advertising
Do Your Own PR
Employ & Manage Staff
Investing in Stocks & Shares
Keep Business Accounts
Manage a Sales Team
Manage an Office
Manage Budgets & Cash Flows
Manage Computers at Work
Manage People at Work

Managing Meetings
Market Yourself
Master Book-Keeping
Master Public Speaking
Prepare a Business Plan
Publish a Book
Publish a Newsletter
Raise Business Finance
Sell Your Business
Start a Business from Home
Start Your Own Business
Taking on Staff
Understand Finance at Work
Use the Internet
Winning Presentations
Write a Report
Write Business Letters
Write & Sell Computer Software

Further titles in preparation

The How To series now contains more than 150 titles in the following categories:

Business Basics
Family Reference
Jobs & Careers
Living & Working Abroad
Student Handbooks
Successful Writing

Please send for a free copy of the latest catalogue for full details (see back cover for address).

Contents

Contents

List of Illustrations

IS THIS YOU?

Accountant   Advertising manager

Bank manager

Building society manager   Building surveyor

Club chairperson

Company secretary   County councillor

Dentist

Director   Doctor

Editor

Estate agent   Firefighter

Hospital administrator

Hotel manager   Housewife

Interviewer

Jury foreman   Managing director

Marketing manager

Nurse   Office manager

Optician

Parent   Parish councillor

Personal assistant

Personnel manager   Politician

Practice manager

Publisher   Quantity surveyor

Sales manager

School governor   Secretary

Self-employed person

Shopkeeper   Solicitor

Student

Teacher   Veterinary surgeon

Preface

Meetings have become a vital part of our everyday life. Whether at home or in business, many of us will be involved in meetings at some time or another. These meetings can be effective or non-effective, depending on their purpose, the amount of planning beforehand, the way they are run, and the willingness of those present to reach a satisfactory conclusion.

By the time a well run meeting ends everyone present knows what is going to happen next and how to go about implementing the decisions/actions that have been discussed. On the other hand, at a badly run meeting, the members feel disinclined to participate, a state of apathy presides and at the end of the meeting everyone feels that the whole exercise has been a waste of time.

Managing Meetings offers a down to earth insight into the entire subject. You will soon see that today's meetings no longer need to be stuffy, or boring. Four case studies are used throughout the book to illustrate the various general points made in each chapter.

Whether you have day-to-day 'chats' with colleagues at work, run your own club or society, or organise large-scale business meetings, *Managing Meetings* should give you the necessary information to enable your future meetings to become enlightening, meaningful occasions, enjoyed by everyone who attends them.

Ann Dobson

1
Let's Have a Meeting

DECIDING WHAT MEETINGS ARE

The dictionary definition of the word meeting is 'a coming together'. In the context of this book we actually mean 'a coming together of people for a specific purpose'.

Every one of us is involved in meetings of one kind or another. They are part of our life. A family discussion over what is going to happen to Aunt Ada when she comes out of hospital is a meeting. A chat with the solicitor who is carrying out the legal work connected to our house move is a meeting. Talking to the teacher at parents evening is a meeting. A meeting involves two or more persons and can be anything from a friendly chat to a full-blown, formal annual general meeting of shareholders from all over the country or world.

When is a meeting not a meeting?

Of course, meetings can sometimes be used as an excuse or a reason not to be interrupted. How many times, for instance, have you telephoned someone, only to be told that he or she 'is in a meeting'? This does not necessarily mean a formal meeting. The person concerned may well be talking to just one person, but the term meeting is still used to describe their conversation. Technically the term is correct, but one-to-one chats may take place all day leaving no time when that person considers themselves 'available' to callers. Not a very satisfactory arrangement!

Days that are full of meetings leave no time for **action**, and meetings are meaningless unless they are followed by positive action. Meetings, held at the appropriate times and conducted effectively, can be very useful, but too many meetings can be counterproductive.

APPRECIATING THEIR IMPORTANCE

None of us can exist without relying in some way or another on

One-to-one chat

Sales meetings

Breakfast/lunch/dinner meeting

Disciplinary meeting

Appraisal meeting

Job interview/meeting

Annual general meeting

Regular business meeting

Committee meeting

'Brainstorming' meeting

Board meeting

Shareholders' meeting

Local authority meeting

Jury meeting

Parliamentary meeting

Meeting in court of law

Public meeting – such as planning, parish council *etc*

Meeting with bank manager/accountant *etc*

Ceremonial meeting – wedding/funeral/presentation *etc*

School/university speech day

PTA meeting

School governors' meeting

Social/sports club meeting

Fig. 1. Examples of different types of meetings.

other people. In the same way, no organisation can exist entirely on its own and meetings are an important way of bringing people together to **communicate** and **inform**.

Understanding the value of meetings

Meetings are especially important for:

- Making people **feel involved**. Because they have been invited to attend the meeting they feel they have a useful part to play.

- Generating a **team spirit**. Most people like to feel part of a team effort rather than being in a 'them and us' situation.

- Passing on **information**. One of the main functions of a meeting is to inform successfully.

- Making difficult **decisions**. Difficult decisions often need careful consideration. Those present at a meeting may have widely differing views to express before that decision is made. As long as these views are constructive rather than destructive the right decision should eventually be reached by group discussion.

- Sharing **problems**. 'A problem shared is a problem halved.' So goes the saying and it is often very true.

- Finding **solutions**. Once the problems have been discussed possible solutions can be suggested by those present at the meeting.

- Generating **new ideas**. Brainstorming is discussed in Chapter 5. This is one of the most effective ways of generating new ideas. Every organisation needs new ideas and suggestions for the future, otherwise it will become stale and out of touch.

- Introducing **new policies**. When new policies are to be introduced into a business organisation, the workforce will accept those new policies more readily if the details are explained to them first.

UNDERSTANDING WHY MEETINGS CAN FAIL

There is a great number of reasons why meetings can fail. Although this might seem a rather negative angle to take, by understanding why they fail, we should be able to work on their success.

Why do some meetings fail?
The most important reasons are:

The meeting was not really necessary in the first place
This is perhaps the most common reason why meetings fail. So often people are brought together, giving up time that could be better spent elsewhere, when a telephone call, or a letter, would have achieved the same result.

Wrong time, wrong place
There are good times and bad times to hold meetings. Friday afternoon in a traditional business environment, for instance, is usually considered to be a very bad time to arrange anything other than an informal 'chat'. For those fortunate enough to work the traditional five day week, Friday afternoon is a winding down time, when thoughts are of the weekend ahead rather than the pressing problems of work.

Just the same as there are good and bad times to hold meetings, there are also good and bad places. An overheated, smoky room will not generate stimulating conversation amongst those present. Neither will an unheated room, or one where the walls and carpet merge together in a depressing dingy selection of colours.

Natural light, adequate heating, pleasant surroundings, refreshments at the right time, comfortable seating and an effective seating plan are all necessary for a meeting to stand a chance of being successful.

Insufficient planning and preparation beforehand
Unless the meeting is just an informal chat between two people, a good deal of planning and preparation needs to take place before the day of the meeting. We will be looking at this planning and preparation in Chapters 8 and 9, but suffice it to say that some form of programme or agenda needs to be formulated, and everyone who is expected to attend the meeting should have adequate notice of the date and time.

Wrong people attending the meeting
It is vitally important to ensure that the correct people are invited to any meeting. Otherwise nothing will be achieved and the meeting will have to be held again at a later date.

Poorly conducted meeting
A meeting needs to be conducted in an orderly fashion. This means keeping to the point and not allowing any deviation from the programme or agenda. If the meeting dissolves into a general 'chit-chat' the proceedings will drag on and on with a completely negative end result.

Disruptions
The constant ring of a telephone will cause disruption and telephone calls should be diverted while the meeting takes place. Similarly, latecomers, those who constantly 'butt in' and participants called away because they have not arranged adequate cover for the meeting, will all prevent the smooth running of the proceedings and should be prevented whenever possible. We discuss troublemakers at meetings in detail in Chapter 7.

ENSURING A PURPOSE

A meeting should always have a **purpose** and everyone attending the meeting should know what that purpose is. This seems a fairly obvious statement, but it is often the case that the person chairing the meeting knows exactly what he or she hopes to achieve, but leaves the participants to play a guessing game.

When a meeting has a definite purpose, apparent to all, then just so long as the programme or agenda is strictly adhered to, the meeting stands a very good chance of achieving its aims.

A meeting without a purpose is like a singer who has no song to sing. One is worthless without the other.

MAKING THINGS HAPPEN

In order to make things happen at a meeting, you as the chairperson or organiser should be:

- good at communicating
- enthusiastic
- positive
- firm.

Good communication skills are very important if you are to be involved with meetings. Although some people are born orators, others have to work at it. If you are naturally shy and lacking in self confidence you may not feel you can cope with managing a meeting successfully. However, after reading Chapters 2–7, you will, hopefully, change your mind!

Enthusiasm is infectious. If you portray an enthusiastic and genuinely positive approach to the matters in hand the chances are other people will feel enthusiastic and positive too. That way, the maximum benefit will be gained from the meeting.

Being firm

Being firm is not always easy. As we have already said, trouble-makers are dealt with in Chapter 7, but a firm hand can still be needed when there are no troublemakers present. It is up to you when managing a meeting to let everyone see that whilst you are quite human and appreciate a joke just as much as the next person, you intend to keep to the subject and finish the meeting with a positive rather than negative outcome.

DOING AWAY WITH MEETINGS OF HABIT

Far too many meetings are held because they have always been held – rather than for a specific purpose. An example of this is the typical weekly sales meeting where all the sales reps have to travel long distances to attend what turns out to be very much a repeat of the meeting they attended the week before. No one knows why the meetings are held. They never really achieve anything, but the lunch is quite nice afterwards. Even the sales manager has forgotten why he calls them all in week after week. Surely the reps' time could be better spent 'on the road', visiting customers and gaining orders, with sales meetings arranged as and when necessary.

Meetings that waste time

Meetings of habit are, largely, a waste of time. Everyone is bored before they even start and no one participates fully because they just can't be bothered. As a result, very little is achieved and, in fact, such meetings can actually have an adverse rather than helpful long-term effect on those who attend.

CASE STUDIES

Throughout the book four case studies are used to illustrate the various points made in each chapter. First, we'll take a look at their background.

Martin

Martin is a 40 year old sales manager of a large pharmaceutical company. He holds regular monthly meetings which all his sales team attend. Martin tends to be a rather aggressive person, who often relies on 'bullying' tactics to get the desired results.

George

George is 52 and runs a successful boatyard which he now operates as a private limited company. They hold formal meetings once a year and plenty of informal ones at the boatyard in between. George believes that meetings form an important part of everyday working life, although he often uses rather unorthodox methods to run them.

Sarah

Sarah is 25 and holds a very demanding position as practice manager for a large group of doctors. She is responsible for the organisation and running of the monthly practice meetings which all the doctors and other senior staff attend. She is a dynamic, go-ahead kind of person, who believes that actions speak louder than words.

Anna

Anna, aged 35, is chairman of the local drama club. The club holds meetings several times a year. Some meetings are held to discuss forthcoming productions and others to appoint committee members and organise fund-raising events. Anna has run the club for ten years and sometimes finds other people's ideas hard to accept.

CHECKLIST

- Do you understand what a meeting is?

- Are you aware of their importance?

- Are your meetings always necessary?

- Do you give sufficient thought to the time and place?

- Do you plan your meetings well in advance? ·

Mr A

36 year old local businessman. Has his own shop in the centre of town. Married with two children at High School.

His meetings during one month:

Meeting with solicitor to discuss house move

Meeting with the local traders association

Meeting with the headteacher at the school

Parent/teachers association meeting

Staff meeting to discuss changes at his shop

Monthly committee meeting at the golf club.

Mrs B

50 year old housewife/part time nurse. Does a lot of work for charity. Married with two married daughters.

Her meetings during one month:

Meeting with doctors treating her mother in hospital

Meeting with social workers over plans to move her mother into a home

Women's Institute committee meeting

WRVS monthly meeting

Cancer Research fund-raising committee meeting

Nurses meeting over pay awards

Hospital trust meeting.

Fig. 2. Meetings and everyday life.

- Do your meetings always have a specific purpose?

- Are you good at making things happen?

- Do you ever hold meetings of habit?

DISCUSSION POINTS

1. 'All organisations need to hold meetings.' Do you consider this statement to be true? Give reasons for your answer.

2. Give ten reasons why you think a meeting could be a waste of time.

3. How much do you think personality plays a part in the running of a meeting?

2
Communicating Effectively at Meetings

SPEAKING CONFIDENTLY

When you are the person involved in managing a meeting of any kind it is very important that you show confidence and complete control of the proceedings.

In order to instil confidence in other people you will need to make sure that you are **fully prepared** for the meeting taking place. Stumbling over your words through nerves is one thing, but stumbling because you do not know what you are supposed to be saying is quite another.

Assuming that you have prepared the necessary information and agenda for the meeting, you will stand a good chance of convincing everyone that the meeting has a purpose and that you are in charge of that purpose.

Tips for the nervous

If you are the nervous type, try the following before the meeting:

- Tell yourself that everything will run smoothly and that you are on top of the situation.

- Quickly run through in your mind the matters being discussed and make sure you have some notes to refer to.

- Try some deep breathing exercises to calm your nerves.

- If the meeting is in your own office, welcome everyone with a confident smile.

- When the meeting is taking place elsewhere, enter the meeting room smiling and talk to those already there, even if it is only to say 'Good morning/afternoon'.

- Don't worry too much if you still feel anxious. The adrenalin tends to flow quicker when you are slightly nervous and you may give a better performance as a result. Once the meeting gets going your nervousness should largely disappear anyway.

Above all, learn to believe in yourself and your ability to cope with every eventuality, but at the same time ensure that you do not sound either dictatorial or patronising when you speak to other people. Never speak as though you are addressing a group of children (unless you are of course!). Adults do not like being spoken down to.

KEEPING THINGS SIMPLE

Meetings used to be very formal affairs with everyone speaking through the chair and only at their allotted times. Although some meetings are still formal, *eg*, annual general meetings of shareholders, the vast majority are now much more 'human', with those present speaking when they wish and addressing their fellow participants by their first names. This helps to make people feel more comfortable and less inhibited.

Simple language can help too. Never use a big word when a small word will do. No one will be impressed with your astonishingly large vocabulary if they cannot understand what you are trying to say. Keep your sentences short. Use 'we' or 'you' rather than 'I' whenever possible, and avoid 'stuffy' terms such as 'lie on the table', 'point of order' *etc*, unless your meeting is a very formal one that calls for such language.

KEEPING THINGS RELEVANT

Before a meeting takes place you should have prepared an **agenda** or list of items that are going to be discussed. It is very important that this list is then followed through in a logical sequence.

Meetings always seem to attract at least one participant who insists on bringing up a subject totally unrelated to the purpose of the meeting. Should this happen to you, be polite but firm, telling the person that the essential matters must be dealt with first, and then if there is time at the end perhaps their topic can be discussed. In reality there is rarely spare time at the end of a meeting, but dismissing the participants out of hand will not help you to manage the rest of the meeting effectively.

UNDERSTANDING GROUP BEHAVIOUR

People behave very differently in groups from the way they behave individually. To begin with, everyone in a group has to speak in front of other people and conflicts of suggestions and ideas are inevitable. It must be remembered too that public speaking can come very hard to some people and in a group situation they may not always say exactly what they really mean for fear of being mocked or laughed at.

Appreciating how newcomers feel

A newcomer to a regularly held meeting will always feel out of place at first and will probably be quiet and reserved. They are also likely to conform and agree with most, if not everything, decided. As that person becomes more familiar with the other participants, he or she will normally begin to feel a part of the group they have joined. Then they will start to put their own point of view on the matters discussed, not necessarily agreeing with everyone else as a matter of course.

On the other hand, a newly set up meeting means that all the participants are new together and, rather like at school, they will gradually begin to find common ground with their fellow 'meeting partners'.

Listening to everyone's opinion

All opinions should be respected rather than dismissed just because they do not fit in with the group, and everyone's particular area of expertise needs to be used to the full. You may be in charge of the meeting, but there could well be people attending who know far more about certain subjects than you do. This is one of the reasons for calling a meeting in the first place – to get an interaction of ideas and information.

Generally speaking, the smaller the meeting, the better the relationship between participants, because they get to know each other and begin to establish a group rapport.

DEALING WITH A POWER STRUGGLE

It is not just in the business world that some people want as much power as possible. Even the local cricket club, which is very low key and insignificant compared to giants like Birds Eye or Shell, has its power seekers.

In the context of meetings the power struggle could take two forms:

- It could be between the chairperson and someone who wants to become that chairperson.

- It could be between participants at the meeting, each out to show that they are better than the others.

If you are the chairperson and someone wants your job, consider first, assuming they are capable, the possibility of actually letting them have it! After all, why should you put up with the aggravation of running meetings if someone else is prepared to take it on their shoulders? On the other hand, you might enjoy your position, in which case you will just have to tell your rival that you are staying put whatever they say or do.

Power struggles between participants at a meeting are inevitable at some time or another. They should be tolerated to an extent, and you should only intervene if the matter gets out of hand. Usually such incidents have a habit of sorting themselves out eventually, although unfortunately they create a big 'yawn' element amongst everyone who is not involved in the private little war.

How to intervene
If and when you do have to intervene it is better to do so outside the actual meeting room. Speak to both parties and explain that they are disrupting the meeting by their constant bickering. They may not realise that they are affecting other people and a gentle reminder is often all that is necessary to calm them down. Should the situation deteriorate further you will have to consider asking the people involved to leave the meeting.

COMMUNICATING WITH INDIVIDUALS

Much of this book is geared towards dealing with the organising and running of meetings involving several people. One-to-one meetings are also a very frequent occurrence in the business world of today, however, and although these are often thought of as less nerve-wracking than larger meetings, communicating effectively with individuals takes just as much time and effort.

Some examples of one-to-one meetings in a working environment could include:

- the job meeting
- the disciplinary meeting
- the redundancy meeting
- the appraisal meeting
- the breakfast/lunch/dinner meeting.

The single most important point to remember when communicating with individuals is to put the other person at their ease. Whatever the reason for holding the meeting you will both gain the maximum amount of benefit if it is conducted in a friendly, approachable way. When the other person feels threatened or uncomfortable he or she will 'clam up' and the meeting will have been a waste of time.

Guidelines for one-to-one meetings
The following are general guidelines for one-to-one meetings:

- **Welcome** the person with a handshake, introduce yourself if necessary, and invite them to sit down.

- Begin with some general **conversation**.

- **Introduce** the matter or matters to be discussed.

- **Talk directly** to the applicant asking as many 'open ended' questions as you can. 'Open ended' questions need more than a one word answer.

- Show a **real interest** in what is being said to you. Nod, smile and use encouraging words.

- **Make notes** as the meeting progresses. Never rely on memory.

- Discuss what is to **happen next**.

- Try to end the meeting on a **reassuring note** and remember to thank the person for attending.

Being a good communicator
Everyone tends to think that communication skills come naturally and do not have to be worked at. They are wrong. Many of us are very poor communicators and as a result no one ever knows what

we are really trying to say. There isn't the time at any kind of meeting to leave anything to chance. 'Say what you mean and mean what you say' sums up what your aims should be if you are to get your message across effectively at your meeting.

CASE STUDIES

Martin loses his temper

Martin has a middle-aged rep called Harry who thinks he knows everything and insists on butting in with irrelevancies to interrupt the flow of the meetings. One day Martin decides he has had enough and the conversation runs as follows:

Martin: Right, so can any of you think of reasons why Bromphene is not selling so well now?

Harry: When I worked in London for Hywell Pharmaceuticals we had a much better drug than Bromphene.

Martin: Well maybe you did, Harry, but that does not solve our present problem, does it?

Harry: In fact Hywell were a jolly good company. I enjoyed my time with them. They were much more generous than this lot.

Martin: Harry, we are trying to discuss the falling sales of Bromphene.

Harry: I got on very well with the sales manager *there*.

Martin: For God's sake *shut up* Harry. The company went bust. You had no option but to leave and you are damn lucky to have got a job with us. Now just shut up and let the rest of us have a decent conversation for a change.

Harry is furious. He tells everyone in the sales office how rude Martin was to him. Martin, not known for his tact and diplomacy, knows he should not have lost his temper, but he has reached the end of his tether. Needless to say, Harry is *very* quiet in future, so Martin achieved his aim, even if he should have shown a little more restraint!

George gets prepared

George is holding his first formal annual meeting. As chairperson he knows he has many responsibilities and duties to perform and he is terrified. Most of his informal meetings have just been with a few directors at a time, but this one will have 15 people attending.

Before the meeting he telephones the hall to check everything is in order. He then goes for a long walk along the river to prepare himself mentally. He runs over in his head what the procedure will be and when he gets back to the yard he checks carefully through all the notes he has made.

When he arrives at the hall, George takes several slow, deep breaths before striding purposefully into the room where the meeting is to be held. A few people have already arrived and he manages to have a laugh and a joke with them which puts him more at ease.

As he stands up to address the meeting for the first time, he knows he is visibly shaking, but ten minutes later he feels he has the situation well under control.

By preparing himself well beforehand, George has gone to the meeting knowing that he *can* cope with everything, even if he does find the thought of all the people rather nerve-wracking.

Sarah makes a plan

Sarah is arranging job interviews for the position of secretary to the district nurses. She has decided to interview six applicants, and prior to their arrival she has written herself a plan to follow. Her plan is:

1. Welcome applicant. Sit them down and offer tea or coffee.

2. Ask the applicant what they know about the practice – to see whether they have been interested enough to do some research.

3. Talk about the practice in general – how many doctors, other medical staff *etc*. Explain what the district nurses do.

4. Explain what the job entails and the special qualities being looked for.

5. Ask applicant why he or she feels they are suitable for this position. Listen carefully to answer given.

6. Ask more general questions about applicant's background, future ambitions, past experiences *etc*. Use the applicant's CV and application form to help with this part.

7. Give them a typing test and assess result.

8. Thank applicant for attending. Ask if they have any questions, then escort them to door.

Total time – 30 minutes maximum.

Sarah seems very well organised for what lies ahead!

Anna retains the chair

Anna has a problem. She has been chairperson of the Boxwood drama club for ten years but now John the treasurer has made it clear that he would like her job, and that she should hand over to someone younger and fresher.

Anna calls a meeting of all the committee members. She tells them about the threat to her leadership in front of John who wants to oust her. They take a vote on it and apart from John everyone wants her to stay, so this restores her confidence.

Anna is a little domineering so it is not surprising that someone has challenged her leadership, but on balance the rest of the committee feel they prefer her to John, who is a real bighead.

CHECKLIST

- Can you speak in a confident way?

- Do you know how to calm any last minute nerves?

- Do you speak in simple language at meetings?

- Are all the points discussed at your meetings relevant?

- Have you thought about the special skills needed when communicating with individuals?

- Can you cope well with one-to-one meetings?

- Are you aware of the underlying feelings amongst groups?

- Can you control members of a group who are a threat to your meetings' success?

DISCUSSION POINTS

1. Think about the differences between conducting a one-to-one meeting and a group meeting. Write down as many as you can.

2. You have someone at your meeting who insists on deviating from the matters being discussed. How would you handle this situation?

3. You are chairman of the local music society. You have a new committee member, who you know is very shy. What could you do and say at the first meeting to make that person feel more at ease?

3
Motivating and Persuading
at Meetings

MOTIVATING YOURSELF

Anyone involved in managing meetings should work very hard at becoming sufficiently motivated and enthusiastic about their task. After all, if you cannot motivate yourself, what chance do you stand of motivating other people?

Motivating yourself to manage your meeting effectively involves:

- Preparation and planning in advance so that you know exactly what form the meeting will take.

- Choosing the correct people to attend your meeting.

- Making sure that the meeting is at a suitable time for everyone, including yourself, to give of their best.

- Adopting a strong element of self-discipline. Maybe you are not too enthusiastic about a meeting to discuss the rising costs of telephone calls in your organisation, but if the meeting is considered necessary, then it should be conducted with the right amount of commitment.

- Speaking to yourself severely before the meeting begins, saying that on no account will you look bored or begin to yawn!

MOTIVATING OTHER PEOPLE

Once you feel motivated then it is up to you to motivate the other participants at the meeting. It has been said by many that the best way to motivate people at a meeting is to tell them that the sooner the business is done the sooner everyone can go down to the pub! Management motivation at its best! The trouble with that theory, however, is that the people most likely to hold up the meeting are the ones who would not go to the pub afterwards anyway.

Being effective
On a more serious note, effective motivation can be achieved by:

* Encouraging involvement from everyone present.

* Sounding interested in what they have to say.

* Showing respect for other people's ideas and suggestions even if they don't coincide with your own.

* Trying to give everyone some responsibility. This can take the form of handing over the proceedings to another person from time to time so that they can explain a particular point, or asking for certain matters to be followed up by individuals after the meeting.

* Not adopting a domineering attitude. Just because you are 'in charge' does not mean that you are better than the rest.

* Making it plain that co-operation and participation from everyone will bring a speedy conclusion to the meeting.

VALUING EVERYONE

All of us need to 'feel needed' and participants at a meeting are no exception. It is up to you to show that every single person at your meeting is of value, although, of course, this is only possible if the right people have been invited to attend in the first place.

Along with our desire to feel needed, we also like to be **recognised** for who we are and what we stand for. In other words we like to make an impression. At meetings everyone should be made to feel both individual as a person, with their own views and ideas, but equal in terms of their value to the meeting.

Saying 'thank you'
Something that many of us are very bad at remembering is to say 'thank you' when another person helps us in some way. To say 'thank you' to those who have assisted, either at the meeting itself,

or beforehand with providing the necessary information, goes a long way towards building up a mutually beneficial working relationship.

Meetings run as a co-operative, with everyone pulling together rather than working alone, are the meetings that achieve their aims. If everyone feels valued and wanted they will then participate fully in the proceedings.

USING GENTLE PERSUASION

Telling someone they should do something they do not want to do generally causes resentment. Gentle persuasion, however, is an art that can be acquired and used to maximum effect.

Persuasion tactics at a meeting can be achieved by:

- putting your case as strongly and clearly as you can

- giving reasons for any conclusions you have come to

- listening to other people's objections and discussing them fully

- aiming to reach a 'negotiated settlement', agreeable to all, although this may involve some degree of compromise.

Let us look at a fictitious example of gentle persuasion in action:

Example: Andrew's club
Andrew is chairing a meeting of the local tennis club. They are discussing where to hold the annual Christmas dinner. Andrew and three of the other members want to use the local hotel – The Grange – whilst the other members think the club hall with outside caterers would be more suitable. The conversation goes like this:

Andrew: Well the decision has to be made between The Grange or the club hall, otherwise it will be too late to arrange anything. Shall I tell you what they are offering us?

John: The Grange is too expensive. You said before it would be £12.00 a head and that is a lot of money to find. If we use our own hall and get in Rosebery Caterers we should be able to do it much cheaper.

Andrew: Do you know what Rosebery would charge, John?

John: Well no, but I could find out.

Andrew: Actually I 'phoned them before the meeting and they quoted me £10.00 a head, so is £2.00 worth saving, considering the more pleasant surroundings at The Grange?

Peter: What about the drinks though? They'll really sting us for those at The Grange.

Andrew: No they won't. I was about to explain about those. They have said they'll do a special deal if we book for the whole club, and let the hotel manager and his family use our tennis courts next summer! They mentioned trade prices, so they can't be fairer than that.

Richard: I agree with Andrew, The Grange are prepared to put themselves out for us and it sounds very reasonable to me. (Murmurs of agreement go around the room.)

Peter: Well, I suppose so. I didn't realise that they would offer us so much. We ought to take a vote on it though.

They do so by a show of hands and everyone agrees to book The Grange. Andrew has done his 'homework' in advance and is able to get his own way without upsetting anyone.

SHOWING COURAGE

Whilst you should never show a domineering attitude at a meeting, neither should you be prepared to be 'walked over' by everyone else. Anyone managing a meeting needs courage, if only to stand up to the other participants. As far as your own suggestions and recommendations are concerned, you may have to compromise, and be prepared to negotiate, but you should still have the courage to stick to your own principles.

Accepting criticism
All of us at some time or another have to accept **criticism** and it may

well be that you will be criticised at a meeting you are managing. There is, however, a big difference between constructive criticism and criticism without any purpose. Constructive criticism can be very helpful. Criticism for no reason is destructive.

If you are criticised, first of all stop and think whether the criticism is justified. If it is, do something about it. Never be afraid to admit that you have made a mistake. We all make mistakes every day of our lives, but only people with courage own up to them.

On the other hand, if you honestly feel the criticism is unjustified then challenge the person involved and ask them why they think you are in the wrong. It is an unfortunate fact of life that some people seem to need to justify themselves by continually criticising others. By challenging them you will make them stop and think, and they will hopefully admit that they were in the wrong, or at least keep quiet in future because they know that you will not stand for their tantrums.

RESOLVING CONFLICT

Resolving conflict within a group can be a very important responsibility for the person managing a meeting. Inevitably some conflict always occurs in a democratic society where everyone is entitled to voice his or her opinions. When that conflict gets out of hand, however, it is imperative that the problem is tackled sooner rather than later, otherwise the meeting will not conclude in a satisfactory way.

1. The conflict may be between yourself and someone else at the meeting, and it may take the form of criticism or just plain nastiness. As we said above, (see Showing Courage) **challenging the person** is usually the best policy.

2. If the conflict is between other participants at the meeting, try to draw the trouble out by **gentle questioning** of the people involved. Never allow situations like this to fester. You do not want feelings of anger or resentment building up to such an extent that they destroy the meeting entirely.

Resolving conflict can be easier than expected. Once everyone has had their say on the matter, they are often satisfied to let the proceedings continue. If not, then take the same action as you would with a power struggle (see Chapter 2) and speak to the people involved outside the meeting room environment, asking them to leave the group if the situation deteriorates further.

CASE STUDIES

Martin times his meetings badly
Martin, being the aggressive type, always starts his sales meetings with the following little speech:

'Right lads and lasses. I don't want to be here any more than you do, so the sooner we get on with the business the sooner we will all be able to go home.'

He plans the meetings for a Friday afternoon and everyone knows that there is no chance of them going until the business has been completed.

By this method Martin does motivate himself and his sales team to get on with the meeting, but the results at the end are not always satisfactory because he has chosen a poor time for the meeting to be held. By Friday afternoon, after a week on the road, the reps have had enough and they will agree to almost anything just to get home for the weekend.

George learns to listen to others
Meetings at the boatyard create few worries for George. Because he has run the yard himself for so many years he has developed a way of persuading everyone present that his ideas are best, and it is rare for anyone to disagree with him, because usually he does know best.

At one meeting, however, someone interrupts him mid-flow and tells him that they think he is wrong on a particular point – that of how many day boats they should replace during the current year. He stops and stares at Bill, the person who has interrupted him, quite shocked that his judgement has been questioned. He asks the other members present what they think and, apart from one, they agree with Bill.

Everything goes deadly quiet. No one wants to upset George because they all like him a lot, but on the other hand they think they are right on this particular point.

George does some quick thinking. He realises that perhaps he was a little hasty and he should have consulted everyone else before 'deciding' on the day boats. He admits he was wrong and that he is quite happy to go along with everyone else's decision on this one.

There is an audible sigh of relief around the room!

Sarah sticks to the agenda

There has for a time been some underlying bickering going on between the district nurses and the practice nurses. At a practice meeting one month the matter comes to a head and one of the district nurses blatantly accuses the practice nurses of treating them unfairly by refusing to let them use their rooms when they need to carry out simple procedures on the health centre premises.

Sarah intervenes. She begins by saying that this is not a matter due for discussion today, but that she is quite prepared to chair a special meeting the following week to discuss the problems of accommodation for the nurses.

This defuses a difficult situation and the meeting is able to continue on course. The nurses are happy because they know their problems will be discussed the following week.

Anna organises a recruitment campaign

The drama club that Anna runs has lost several of its members. A variety of reasons such as people moving away, getting married and finding other interests *etc*, have all contributed to the present situation.

Anna calls a meeting of the entire club to discuss the problem. She impresses on everyone the need to help with the recruiting of more members. She asks for volunteers to deliver leaflets in the area telling people about the club and what it has to offer.

By involving all the club members and making them feel important, Anna gets the response she requires. Almost everyone agrees to help in whatever way they can. A couple even volunteer to visit the local school's sixth form and college to speak to the students and try to persuade them to join.

As a result of this joint effort, new members flood to the club and within three months it is back to full strength once more.

CHECKLIST

- Are you a well-motivated person? If not, how are you going to change?

- Do you show respect and enthusiasm for other people's ideas and suggestions?

- Are you prepared to offer everyone some responsibility?

- Do you say 'thank you' to someone when they have been of value to you or your fellow participants?

- Have you learnt the art of gentle persuasion?

- Are you prepared to admit when you are wrong?

- Can you resolve any conflict that arises during the course of a meeting?

DISCUSSION POINTS

1. Do you think self-motivation is important where meetings are concerned? Give reasons for your answer.

2. How can you show people that you value their opinions, suggestions and help at your meetings?

3. How can you stop internal bickering at a meeting?

4
Problem-Solving at Meetings

IDENTIFYING THE PROBLEM

Problems, problems everywhere! It is true to say that our lives, whatever form they take, are always full of problems. In fact, at times it seems we have so many problems that they all get mixed up together and none of them gets solved. When this happens, the problems themselves get larger, our stress levels rise, and the vicious circle goes on and on.

At meetings it is vitally important that any problems being discussed are identified straight away and that each problem is treated as a separate issue. As the person managing the meeting it is up to you to take one problem at a time, explaining the details, and then encouraging the other participants to think about a possible solution.

To make the various stages of problem-solving easier to understand we look at a fictitious organisation – a hotel and their monthly meeting. This month they are discussing one particular problem, before moving on to the other routine business.

Identifying the problem at The Queens Hotel

The chairperson, Paul Jones, opens the meeting by welcoming everybody, going through the absences and then signing the minutes of the last meeting. Once that is out of the way he proceeds to the next item on the agenda and identifies the problem to be discussed as follows:

'Ladies and gentlemen, we have a particularly worrying problem to deal with here this evening. Over the last six months we have seen the takings in our restaurant drop by almost a half. This is obviously having a detrimental effect on the finances of the entire hotel and cannot be allowed to continue.'

He goes on:

'I shall now call on Miss Hunt to explain what she sees to be the causes of this serious situation.'

LOOKING AT THE CAUSES

Problems always occur for a reason, and this is usually because a change of some kind has taken place. Once you and the other participants at the meeting have acknowledged this fact, you will then need to identify the causes for that change.

Something you may well have to overcome at the outset is people's natural resistance to any kind of change. We all feel threatened by the very word 'change', and tend to resent its effect on us. Of course, sometimes the 'change' is for the better, but whether or not this is the case, change has to be accepted and dealt with in a positive way, first by you and then by your participants.

Causes of the problem at The Queens Hotel

Sally Hunt, the hotel manager, rises and explains the background to the problem:

'I have sought the views of many people, some of whom are here today and some not, and the opinion is that we have two main causes of this particular problem:

'Firstly, about eight months ago, as you will all know, the Regency Palace opened at the other end of Brancaster. It opened amidst a blaze of publicity and is part of a well-known chain of hotels, whereas our hotel is privately owned and therefore does not have the same financial backing. The Regency offered cut-price meals for the first few months, and by the time the offers ended it had proved to be a very popular eating place because of its reasonable prices and adventurous menu.

'Secondly, at around the same time The Queens stopped offering its bargain-break weekends which used to contribute considerably to the hotel restaurant's income.

'It would therefore seem reasonable to assume that these are the two contributory causes to the drop in restaurant takings at The Queens.'

Sally sits down and everyone considers what has been said and what can be done about it.

FINDING SOLUTIONS

As we said before, 'a problem shared is a problem halved', and nowhere is this more true than at meetings. Once each problem and its causes have been identified, everyone present at the meeting should be encouraged to offer their ideas on possible solutions.

Solutions to problems will only be found if the chairperson encourages active discussion. No solution to a problem should be dismissed out of hand. Every participant needs to feel that they are being taken seriously.

Solutions to the problem at The Queens Hotel
Various suggestions to solve the problem were then put forward:

1. Paul Jones, the chairperson, suggested reinstating the bargain-break weekends.

2. James Wyatt, the catering manager, suggested a massive advertising campaign, on local radio and in the press, offering special discounts for restaurant meals taken at certain times of the week.

3. Suzy Payne, one of the receptionists, suggested that the menu should be changed. She thought that instead of the present *à la carte* selection, a carvery could be introduced, with limited choices of starters and desserts.

4. Andy Cole, the restaurant manager, told the members present that he had been investigating the possibility of offering a special lighter menu selection at lunchtimes, to cater for those people who did not want to eat a three or four course full meal.

All these possible solutions were discussed, one at a time, by everyone present.

CHOOSING THE BEST ALTERNATIVES

With some problems there is only one solution and unless that is adopted the problem will not be solved.

Most problems, however, have a number of possible solutions, and each one will need to be considered. Once the best alternatives have been decided upon they should be put into effect as soon as possible. Then set a date for another meeting to be held in the future to monitor progress.

The best alternatives for The Queens Hotel
After considerable debate, everyone decided on three solutions to

the problem under discussion:

1. Advertising in the newspapers, including vouchers offering money off restaurant meals, for a trial period of two months.

2. Adopting the restaurant manager's idea of introducing a lighter selection lunchtime menu at reasonable prices.

3. Reinstating the bargain-break weekends, with reduced rates during the winter months.

By identifying the problem, looking at the causes, discussing possible solutions and deciding on the best alternatives, The Queens is able to put into action these various measures which will, hopefully, solve the problem of their falling restaurant takings.

AVOIDING UNNECESSARY PROBLEMS

To some people, especially those with spare time on their hands, everything is a problem which has to be discussed, deliberated on, discussed again and, perhaps, finally resolved. We all know those who are intent on 'making mountains out of molehills'. The less charitable of us will probably say: 'They need something to *really* worry about, then they'd see sense'. Busy people, with full and active lives, tend to be more selective over the problems they take on board.

Is a meeting necessary?

If you are considering holding a meeting just to discuss one specific problem, then the first question to ask yourself is whether that problem is important enough to necessitate taking up the valuable time of several people. Meetings involving a group of people should never be held unless they are absolutely necessary, and unless no other viable means of quicker discussion is available, *eg*, telephone call or brief one-to-one chat.

Always take care to see that first you are not inventing problems where they do not exist and, secondly, that if the meeting does take place, extra problems are not introduced by other participants whilst the first problem is still being sorted out. Too many problems usually result in too few solutions.

CASE STUDIES

Martin decides on two solutions

Martin's problem is that the sales of another of the company's drugs – Tromidene – have fallen dramatically. This is because of some bad publicity when someone died after using it. Although it was proven that the drug was not to blame, sales are still well down. Various solutions to the problem are offered when Martin calls a special meeting with his reps. These include:

1. A special advertising campaign emphasising the good points of the drug, to include free gifts such as pens, clocks *etc*, advertising Tromidene.

2. A letter to be sent to all the GPs and hospital doctors asking them to continue using the drug.

In the end Martin decides to implement both of these ideas, sending the advertising material and free gifts with the letters.

George reduces his fleet

George's problem concerns part of the bank close to the boatyard which does not actually belong to them, but which they have been using to moor up a few of their boats for many years. The actual owner of the bank has said he now wants to use this stretch for his own extended hire-fleet.

George calls a meeting to discuss this problem and the following suggestions are put forward:

1. To ask whether any of the other boatyards in the area would be willing to rent out part of their bank.

2. To cut down the fleet by four or five boats so that the problem of mooring the extra boats would no longer arise. The boats to be sold would be the older two berth models which were getting very old anyway.

3. To take over a stretch of bank close to one of the shareholder's businesses further up river. This stretch could be used for the boats least likely to be fully occupied all season, but it would mean moving them to the main boatyard each time they were to go out on hire.

After much discussion it was decided that four boats should be sold to eliminate the problem of extra bank space being needed.

Sarah finds the best alternative

The receptionists have reported to Sarah that they are no longer able to accommodate all the pregnant women in the maternity clinics being run at the practice. This is because, first, the numbers have increased and, secondly, two of the doctors combined their clinic into one session a couple of years ago.

At a practice meeting, Sarah raises this problem and prompts the following suggestions:

1. That Dr Rowe and Dr Jones start to hold separate clinics again.

2. That a doctor should be recruited just to hold two maternity clinics each week.

Although the better alternative appears to be the first one, Dr Rowe states that he does not feel able to take on his maternity clinic again due to back problems, which is why he combined with Dr Jones in the first place. Everyone therefore decides that the better plan will be for someone to be recruited to take two maternity clinics each week.

Anna solves the 'men shortage' problem

Anna's drama club's next play is *Julius Caesar* and she finds that they do not have enough men to play all the male parts. This is because a number of men have left between choosing the play and rehearsals beginning.

Anna calls a meeting and the following solutions to the problem are offered:

1. Put an advert in the paper asking for men to come forward to act in this one play, if they do not want to actually join the club.

2. Ask three or four of the female members of the club to play male parts.

3. Get certain people to 'double up' on parts where they do not have to be on stage at the same time.

On balance everyone decides that it would be far easier to use the existing members of the club, asking three or four female members to play male parts. If they refuse then the next option will be to try to 'double up' some of the minor parts.

CHECKLIST

- Can you identify the problem or problems to be solved?

- Do you know what the causes are?

- Are you prepared to accept and deal with change?

- Do you deal with problems one at a time?

- Do you listen to other people's solutions to problems?

- Can you identify the best alternatives and put them into action?

- Are you sure that you do not create unnecessary problems?

DISCUSSION POINTS

1. 'Problems always involve people.' What do you understand by this statement and do you consider it to be true?

2. Using your imagination, assume that your village school is to close down and you are trying to keep it open. You chair a meeting of local residents. What do you imagine would be said, to fit under the following headings:

   Problem
   Causes
   Solutions
   Best alternative

3. How important do you think problem-solving meetings are? Do you think they are more or less important then meetings held to implement new policy or talk about new ideas?

5
Generating Ideas at Meetings

BEING CREATIVE

The dictionary defines the word 'create' as 'to bring into existence out of nothing', or 'to originate'. If you are a creative person you will:

- constantly come up with new ideas
- be prepared to put your ideas into effect
- think about different angles to your ideas
- motivate others with your enthusiasm
- keep the meeting 'alive'
- plan for future meetings.

A creative person will know what he or she wants to achieve and will set about realising that aim at any cost. On the other hand, a more logically minded person will think ideas through from A to Z, only proceeding from each stage if the idea still seems feasible.

Managing creatively

Being creative in the context of meetings means having **original ideas** and thoughts to contribute. A meeting with no creativity and an abundance of logic will be a very boring affair, and if you are managing the meeting, it is up to you to be creative yourself and to encourage all the other participants to be creative as well.

In general, creative people get more done. They tend to be the 'high flyers' and 'risk takers', somehow knowing that most of the time they will be successful. There is a very true saying: 'You get out of life what you put into it'. If you can show creativity at meetings you might not succeed in your aims every single time, but when you do, the results will be well worth the wait.

ENCOURAGING IDEAS FROM OTHER PEOPLE

Unless you are having a meeting all on your own, it is not just your ideas that need to be expressed. You might like to think that, being in charge, your ideas are the best, but if you really think that then there is not much point in having a meeting in the first place.

Encourage your fellow participants to put forward their ideas too. Make them feel that their creative influence will be of use, and when ideas are forthcoming, never dismiss them out of hand because they are different from your own. Aim for uninhibited thoughts from everyone. After all, the more ideas put forward on a particular topic, the more constructive discussion can take place, and ultimately the more chance there will be of deciding to implement the right ideas in the end.

ORGANISING IDEAS

Ideas and suggestions put forward at traditional meetings should always be voiced at the appropriate time, and this is achieved by keeping to the correct order as shown on the programme or agenda. For instance, it is no use discussing ideas to do with item 6 on the agenda when item 2 has not yet been dealt with. Any deviations from the agenda will result in lack of interest on the part of the participants, because they will no longer be able to follow what is going on.

In an attempt to ensure that the meeting proceeds in an orderly fashion, therefore, it is useful to set some ground rules. First everyone will need to be told that they must restrict their ideas to the topic under discussion. You can then encourage one person to speak at a time so that any ideas put forward can be discussed and noted. Once that person has finished, someone else can offer their ideas and so on. If this method is adopted the participants will be able to follow through the various topics in a consistent manner, which will in turn help with the decision-making process later on. It will also ensure that the quiet ones get a chance to have their say, rather than just their loudmouth colleagues. In reality, it is often the quiet participants who generate the best ideas, because they think before they open their mouths!

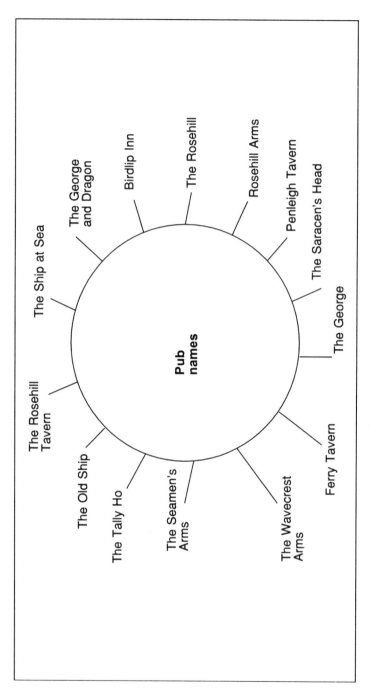

Fig. 3. Brainstorming spider chart.

The George and Dragon

Birdlip Inn

The Rosehill

The Ship at Sea

Rosehill Arms

Penleigh Tavern

The Saracen's Head

Pub names

The George

The Rosehill Tavern

The Old Ship

The Tally Ho

The Seamen's Arms

The Wavecrest Arms

Ferry Tavern

BRAINSTORMING

Instead of holding a traditional type of meeting to generate new ideas, a more recent innovation is the brainstorming session. This type of informal meeting has become very popular, as it encourages increased creativity and forward thinking. Brainstorming can also be an effective way of **solving problems** – see Chapter 4.

How brainstorming works
The way a brainstorming session works is as follows:

- Notification is sent in advance explaining the purpose of the brainstorming session.

- Once the session begins there should be no chairperson or leader taking charge. Someone will need to record the proceedings but everyone should think of themselves as part of a team effort.

- The participants put forward their ideas in connection with the matter being discussed. They do not have to wait their turn as at a traditional meeting.

- These ideas are then shortened to a few key words which are written down by someone in a haphazard fashion on a piece of paper or a flip chart. A well organised person may set the ideas out in the form of a spider chart – see Figure 3 on page 48.

- It should be noted that no one should offer criticism or judgement on any ideas at this stage.

- Once all the ideas have been recorded the team sorts them out into some sort of reasonable order, following which they are looked at in more detail.

- Any ideas that are seen to be of immediate use can be adopted and implemented.

- Other ideas that may be of use in the future can be recorded and filed away in the appropriate place.

To be successful, brainstorming meetings need to be organised as informal gatherings, in as relaxed an environment as possible. If the conditions are right they can be both good fun and of tremendous benefit.

MAKING DECISIONS

If a meeting of any kind is to be a success, decisions will have to be made. Just because you are managing the meeting, you should not think that you will also be responsible for all the decision-making. Often the proposer of the topic under discussion will make the final decision on that particular matter. Sometimes the person who needs to take a final decision will not even be present at the meeting, in which case the decision will have to be deferred.

Ending the meeting with a decision

Whenever possible, however, decisions should be taken on the key topics discussed by the end of the meeting. Meetings have been known to occur week after week and month after month, discussing exactly the same things, purely because *nobody* got around to making decisions on the matters discussed. This situation results in a considerable waste of valuable time and a loss of patience amongst the participants.

Everyone at a meeting is there to share their ideas and their recommendations. Decision-making should be the end result of this group discussion. Good decision-making depends on the following:

● Assembling the facts relating to the decision to be made.

● Identifying the choices available.

● Discussing the matter with the participants at the meeting.

● Considering the 'risk factor'. What will happen if the wrong decision is taken?

● Selecting the option with the lowest risk factor, as long as it still satisfies the aim.

● Never making 'rash' or 'on the spot' decisions that you might regret later on.

It is useful practice for life in general to become a decisive person.

A decisive person gets things done. An indecisive person just thinks about getting things done! We all know 'ditherers' who can never decide on anything. Make sure that you are a positive person, able to make decisions and act on them accordingly.

STANDING BY UNPOPULAR DECISIONS

People who make the decisions at meetings are not always popular. In fact, you will no doubt have to make some decisions that will prove to be decidedly unpopular. It may be that the topic under discussion has been raised by you and after discussion you are the one who needs to give the final verdict. Or perhaps an equal vote has been taken on someone else's proposal and you, as chairperson, are left with the casting vote.

Having made your decision, it is up to you to stand by your convictions. If you have followed the points listed above before making that decision then you should be confident that you have reached the right verdict. We are all different people, however, with different viewpoints on a whole range of subjects, and unfortunately it will only be on rare occasions that everyone present at a meeting will unanimously agree on a particular topic. Those who do not agree with what you have decided will just have to get used to the idea that you were the person who needed to make the decision, and having made it, that it will stand, whether they like it or not.

Whenever you get really fed up about being criticised for decisions you have made, think about our politicians. They never ever seem to make a decision that pleases us all, and yet they survive and develop thick enough skins to withstand their critics. With practice and a little give and take at times, you can learn to do the same!

GETTING REAL

Whilst we sit in our ivory towers working out our meetings to absolute perfection, it is easy to forget that we are just a very small part of a very large world. In the business sense our world is changing rapidly, almost daily, and meetings along with everything else are having to change too.

There is, undoubtedly, a definite move away from formal, stuffy meetings towards the more casual 'chatting' kind of meeting. It also seems that at long last people are beginning to realise that meetings take a considerable amount of time to prepare, run and attend, and often that time could be spent in a more profitable way.

Keeping in touch with reality

So, it is very important to keep in touch with reality, and meetings should only be held for a **specific purpose** such as to generate new ideas or for problem-solving, and at a time and place to suit all the participants.

That said, when you prepare the items for discussion at your meeting, take care to see that you are preparing a realistic and relevant agenda. People cannot afford to waste their time on irrelevancies and if the participants at your meeting feel they have been brought in under false pretences, they are not likely to be in the mood to discuss their ideas.

'Getting real' also involves making everyone feel 'at home' and comfortable. Happy people are infectious and will create a good atmosphere. Unfortunately, unhappy people are infectious too, and your meeting will be doomed to disaster if your participants are unhappy about the way the meeting is going. The only ideas that will be generated then will revolve around how they can best make their escape!

CASE STUDIES

Martin has his confidence undermined

Martin has an increasingly worrying situation to cope with. A new assistant manager called Paul has been appointed by the sales director. This assistant manager has a real creative flair and at the sales meetings he constantly comes up with new ideas and suggestions to deal with the various points and suggestions raised. What is worrying to Martin is that Paul's ideas are usually good ones, which meet with great enthusiasm from the rest of the team.

Paul becomes a popular spokesman because everyone is fed up with Martin's aggressive and dogmatic approach towards them. They do not like being *told* what to do in the same way as a teacher instructs his pupils. Until Paul joined the team, however, they used to take the easy way out and go along with Martin's rather jaded ideas, but now they realise that fresh ideas and a creative mind could help them all to improve their performance. Martin begins to feel increasingly undermined.

George plans an unusual meeting

Everyone knows that George acts in a rather unorthodox way at times, but his latest idea seems particularly unusual. He has notified the other members of the board that he intends to hold a meeting on board one of the hire cruisers. The aim of the meeting is to discuss improvements to be made to their fleet of boats. He thinks that by cruising up and down the river everyone will be able to see the modifications and improvements being made to their competitors' cruisers, so that a definite decision can be made on work to be carried out during the coming winter months. He fully intends Baxters Cruisers to be the market leaders in luxury and extra comforts and hopes that the other board members will agree with him.

Sarah makes an unpopular decision

At a practice meeting Sarah seeks permission to hold regular training sessions for the administrative staff. The doctors agree that she can hold these sessions, as she has requested, every Saturday afternoon between 2pm and 4pm, and all the staff will be asked to attend on a rota basis. When Sarah tells the staff they are furious about having their weekends spoilt by work. Sarah realises that holding these sessions will never be a popular move, but the staff do need extra training and she thinks her decision was the right one to make.

Anna gets everyone thinking

Anna organises a brainstorming session to get some ideas for fund-raising events. They all sit at a big round table and everyone has their own piece of paper to write their ideas on. Anna collects these in, together with her own, and reads out the results to everybody. They take votes on the various suggestions, eventually deciding to hold a sponsored walk and a jumble sale because these two ideas receive the most votes. The remaining ideas are typed up and filed away for future reference. At the end of the meeting everyone feels that they have contributed in some way and that their ideas have been listened to.

CHECKLIST

- Are you a creative or a logical person?

- Do you think you can make yourself more creative and adventurous?

- Do you have original ideas to contribute to your meetings?

- Are you realistic about the type of meetings you need to hold?

- Are you absolutely sure that your meetings are always necessary?

- Do people feel 'at home' when they attend your meetings?

- Can you organise ideas into the correct order and deal with one idea at a time?

- Have you tried brainstorming sessions and, if so, do they work well?

- Are you good at making decisions?

- Do you consult with everyone else before making decisions?

- Are you capable of standing by unpopular decisions?

DISCUSSION POINTS

1. How important do you think it is to follow the programme prepared for a meeting in the correct order?

2. What would you do and say if you made an unpopular decision and everyone affected asked you to think again?

3. How would you define a creative person? List six qualities that you would expect a creative person to possess.

6
Using Body Language at Meetings

UNDERSTANDING BODY LANGUAGE

Body language, sometimes known as **non-verbal communication**, refers to the way we communicate by using different parts of our body rather than the written or spoken word. It is very often the way in which we show the emotional side of our relationships with others. The messages we convey can be deliberate, such as a nod of the head, a smile, a grimace, a shrug of the shoulders – or involuntary such as a shiver.

It is often said that body language can convey more meaning than any words that may be spoken. On the face of it, this could be taken to mean that we are wasting our time saying anything at a meeting, we can just use our body language, but of course this is not the case. Effective body language works alongside our spoken words in order to convey exactly the meaning we require.

GIVING POSITIVE SIGNALS

If you are to give positive signals at a meeting you manage, remember the following:

- Make sure you **arrive on time**, looking unflustered and in control.

- Show to yourself and others that you are **committed to the aims** of the meeting.

- **Show interest** in what is being said.

- Ensure that there will be **no interruptions** from people popping their heads round the door, or the telephone ringing.

It is also very important for you to give the right impression by the way that you look and dress. Turning up in outrageous clothes with your hair dyed pink and blue will probably leave a lasting impression of your unorthodox appearance but not of the meeting itself. Everyone will be so busy looking at you that they will be unable to concentrate on the matters being discussed.

Communicating effectively

When you are addressing a meeting always look at **everyone**. Do not single out one or two participants and focus your eyes solely on them as you speak. This will make the chosen few feel awkward and victimised, whilst the other participants will wonder whether they need to be there at all.

Whilst you are moving your eyes around the room, remember to **smile** occasionally. Even if the meeting is being held to discuss a very serious issue, you still want to build up a rapport with everyone and you will not do this by looking stony-faced and cross all the time. Also, make sure your face always shows the emotion you want it to show even though this might sometimes mean hiding your true feelings.

Take care not to overuse **gestures** such as throwing your arms around to emphasise important points or banging your fists on the table. Such gestures may go down well at party conferences, but they can be a little over the top for the average meeting.

The tone of your **voice** can be a very important way of giving positive or negative signals. A calm, unflustered voice, with a variation of tone and pitch, will hold everyone's interest. Speaking hurriedly and nervously or in a monotonous drone will have the opposite effect. You must sound in control of the situation at all times. Once you falter, the effectiveness of the meeting will be lost.

Finally, try not to yawn or, even worse, 'nod off'. This has been known to happen at meetings, and whilst it is an effective way of bringing the meeting to a hurried close, it is not to be recommended for a successful outcome!

INTERPRETING SIGNALS FROM OTHERS

In the same way as other people can learn a lot about you by watching the way you manage your meeting, so you can watch the other participants and accurately assess their thoughts and feelings, even if they say nothing at all.

The most important signals to look for are as follows:

Eye contact

People who look at you are likely to be listening to what you are saying. Those who look away when you address them are either nervous or have something to hide.

Body direction

In a normal meeting situation everyone sits facing the chairperson. If someone turns their body away they are not impressed with what is happening. Changing direction completely, *eg*, by standing up and pushing back the chair, shows an even greater degree of dissatisfaction.

Posture

Posture can be interpreted in many different ways. For instance, at a meeting, lounging back in a chair does not necessarily show lack of interest in what is being discussed, in the same way as it would in say a classroom situation. Informal meetings are meant to be relaxed affairs and everyone sitting on the edge of their seats may actually indicate fear rather than keen interest in the proceedings. More formal meetings do call for more formal posture, but even then people should not feel they have to sit bolt upright and face the front at all times in order to be taken seriously.

Head movements

The obvious head movements we make are nodding and shaking. Most of us will nod or shake our head in agreement or disagreement almost without consciously thinking, and you will learn a lot from the participants if you watch for these natural reactions to the items being discussed.

Facial expressions

Facial expressions such as smiling or frowning can tell us a great deal. If we concentrate hard we can make sure that we always smile, frown or show a questioning look at the right times. In a meeting, however, these expressions, like nodding and shaking, can often be unconscious.

Gestures

Is someone constantly scratching their head or picking their teeth, or biting their finger nails? Do you have a 'tapper' or a person who shifts about in the seat all the time? All of these gestures suggest nervousness or anxiety, and you should be on your guard, so that you can handle the person with tact and understanding.

Watching and observing everyone at your meeting can be a fascinating pastime. The only danger is that you will spend so much time trying to work out what makes them all 'tick' that you will lose interest in managing the actual formalities of the meeting itself!

CREATING YOUR OWN SPACE

We all need our own space in life. We talk about space as meaning both our personal time and our personal territory. It is up to us to create our own personal time and everyone's needs are different in this respect. Some of us like to spend a good deal of time on our own, whilst others like as much company as they can possibly get.

The importance of space at work

In a working environment our territory space is related to status. The higher up the working ladder you go, so your space will increase. The top executive will generally have a spacious office or even a suite of offices, whilst the poor little clerk will probably only have the space that he or she actually occupies with a desk and chair. At home we tend to erect a fence around our property to show everyone that it belongs to us, and that they are to 'keep out' unless invited in.

Space is also important when it comes to business relationships. How close you stand to a business colleague will suggest how well you know them. If someone moves closer to you than you think is appropriate, you will probably object and become tense, wondering why they are acting in such a way.

Space as far as meetings are concerned largely centres around where you sit in relation to the other participants, and this in turn depends on the formality of the proceedings. If you are the chairperson at a very formal meeting you will usually sit either at the head of the table or at a separate table, setting you apart from the rest, and showing that you are 'in charge'. At an informal meeting your aim should be to create an atmosphere of informality and equality, so sitting amongst the other participants will show that you are 'one of them'.

CONTROLLING AN ATTITUDE PROBLEM

You have probably heard the expression, 'Oh, he/she has an attitude problem'. What exactly do we mean? The dictionary defines 'attitude' as 'a way of thinking and behaving'. An attitude problem therefore means that the person in question thinks and behaves in a manner that is unacceptable to others.

Do you have an attitude problem?

Is it just possible that *you* could have an attitude problem? If you do, you will need to do something about it, otherwise you will not gain the respect of other participants at your meetings.

Check your attitude for yourself:

- Do you resent being told what to do?

- Do you resent being told how to do something, even if you don't know how to do it yourself?

- Do you resent authority in any shape or form?

- Did you dislike being told what to do at school?

- Do you turn up late for meetings, dress inappropriately, and treat everyone else as a 'second class citizen'?

If you have answered 'yes' to at least four of these questions, then you probably do have an attitude problem that other people will have noticed by watching your body language as well as listening to what you have to say.

Once an attitude problem takes a hold it can be very difficult to break. The following suggestions could help to sort it out:

- First, identify why you feel the need to 'kick' against everyone. This might go back to your childhood. A child from an unstable background, or one who has had to compete with extrovert brothers and sisters, can often develop such an attitude problem.

- Next, ask yourself what you are gaining from your actions.

- If you feel you do have something to gain, then fine, carry on as you are. On the other hand, if you are honest with yourself and see that your attitude to others is getting you nowhere, then make up your mind that it is time for a change.

- Next time you manage a meeting, try to adopt a more

approachable attitude, treating everyone in a more friendly way than you have in the past.

- After the meeting, assess the results, which will, hopefully, make you feel more positive about keeping to your new approach.

When you have managed to 'kick the habit' you will become a more respected and liked person. This in turn will make your meetings more enjoyable and rewarding.

CASE STUDIES

Martin changes his approach

There is no doubt in anyone's mind about Martin and his attitude problem. When he was a child, Martin was badly treated by his stepfather and ever since he has had a chip on his shoulder. His aggressive and dictatorial approach at meetings depresses everyone and at the end of it all even Martin isn't particularly pleased with himself.

One day Martin's wife comes along to the sales meeting to take notes on a special matter. She can hardly believe the way that Martin treats his reps and afterwards she tells him so. As an outsider, she is able to see that they all loathe the meetings because they know that they will be talked down to and treated like little boys.

After a very heated discussion Martin agrees to try and change his approach. At the next meeting the reps can hardly believe what they are hearing. He begins by praising them for their efforts over the past few months and then proceeds to actually involve them in the meeting, treating them as equals rather than far beneath him. The results speak for themselves. The reps work harder and start to look forward to their meetings rather than dread them. Martin begins to enjoy his work more too, rather liking the respect he is now receiving from everyone else.

George works on his body language

George's body language sometimes causes him a problem. If he is bored it shows. Most of the meetings he holds are fairly brief and to the point, but he has one member of the board, Adrian, who rambles on and on at every available opportunity. Unfortunately for George, Adrian is a major shareholder.

George realises that he has just got to put up with this irritating little man, although he does try to limit the discussions whenever he can. Instead of yawning behind his hand and fidgeting in his seat, by working hard to appear interested, smile occasionally, and even laugh at the very poor jokes Adrian makes at regular intervals, George feels he is doing all he can to cope with a difficult situation.

Sarah is understanding

Some patients' notes have gone missing and Sarah holds a meeting with the reception staff to find out if anyone knows anything about them. Everyone denies all knowledge of their whereabouts, but Cindy, one of the junior receptionists, sits through the whole meeting staring at the floor and refusing to take part in any of the discussions, her body language pointing to her feelings of guilt.

After the meeting Sarah takes Cindy on one side and asks her gently whether she has seen the notes. She explains that Cindy will not be punished in any way, just so long as the notes are found. Cindy admits to seeing the missing notes in one of the doctor's drawers, but says she did not want to say anything as she should not have been looking in the drawers in the first place.

It turns out that Cindy was looking for Dr Andrews' visiting list which had also gone missing. Dr Andrews is very forgetful and he must have slipped the notes in his drawer by mistake.

Sarah tells Cindy not to worry and that she quite understands. They often have to sort Dr Andrews out and Sarah is convinced that Cindy was not trying to do anything wrong.

Anna's group is aware of their body language

Anna and her drama club are well used to body language. They use it all the time in their acting, so they are easily able to interpret the body language shown by each other off the stage. Because of this, everyone tries very hard to give the right signals at their meetings, knowing full well that any negative body language will be immediately picked up.

CHECKLIST

- Do you know what body language is all about?

- Are you aware that it is as important a means of communicating as the words that we speak?

- Are you able to convey your meaning by the use of body language?

- Do you adopt positive body language for your meetings?

- Are you able to interpret other people's body language?

- Can you work out the amount of territory space you need for your meetings?

- Do you give thought to equality of space at informal meetings?

- Do you have an attitude problem?

- If so, what do you intend to do about it?

DISCUSSION POINTS

1. What part do you see body language playing at meetings?

2. How would you deal with someone falling asleep at one of your meetings?

3. Do you know someone with an 'attitude problem'? Why do you think they act the way that they do?

7
Dealing with Troublemakers

When a very formal meeting is held everyone speaks 'through the chair' and the entire affair is very refined and proper – at least most of the time! Nowadays, however, the majority of meetings are informal with everyone feeling far less reserved and often on first name terms. Although this encourages constructive, free discussion, it also means that there will be a minority of participants who do not 'toe the line' and insist on disrupting the proceedings.

In this chapter we take a look at a selection of potential troublemakers who just might decide to attend your meeting.

THE LATECOMER

There may be unavoidable circumstances that result in a person arriving late at a meeting. Late arrivals disturb everyone, but assuming the reason is genuine you will just have to accept the apology that will hopefully be offered. If a person consistently arrives late, then their lateness is usually avoidable and will merit different treatment.

Action to take

For a 'first offence' give a summary of the proceedings so far, enabling **the latecomer** to pick up on any important points that he or she has missed.

If someone is consistently late, by summarising the proceedings each time they eventually arrive you are making them feel that they do not have to make an effort to be on time. For the 'persistent offender' you could either try looking at the clock pointedly as the latecomer enters the room, halt the meeting entirely until they have sat down and then continue the meeting without summarising the proceedings, which should embarrass them sufficiently for the situation not to arise again. Otherwise you could take them on one side after the meeting and explain that the situation cannot continue because it causes disruption to everyone else and appeal to their better nature to make more of an effort in the future.

THE EARLY LEAVER

Rather like the latecomer, this could be just a 'one off' situation or a repeated episode.

Action to take
Assuming that you know the person is going to be leaving early, and they do not make a habit of it, try to finish the main business of the meeting by the time they have to leave. You can then summarise and deal with odds and ends afterwards.

If someone suddenly announces they are leaving, there is really not much that you can do, apart from notifying them after the meeting of anything important that was said following their departure.

THE SILENT SORT

This is the person who just sits and says absolutely nothing, even though you expect some kind of contribution from them. **The silent sort** can make everyone else feel awkward, so every effort should be made to bring them into the meeting.

Action to take
The action really depends on the cause. If you think the person is just shy or unsure, saying something like: 'Sue, can you tell us about your department's new computer system?' By saying the person's name first you will attract their attention and you should get an answer. Persist if 'Sue' goes quiet again.

Another reason for silence can be that the person does not think they will be taken seriously if they do speak. In this case they need to be told that you and everyone else would value their input on a particular matter.

THE CHATTERBOX

Just the opposite, of course, to the silent sort. **The chatterbox** may contribute too much to the meeting or, even worse, may sit and talk incessantly to his or her next-door neighbour.

Action to take

If the **chatterbox** is talking to a neighbour, a polite: 'Was there something you wanted to say, John? I couldn't quite hear you,' will usually work. Should the person be so thick-skinned that they do not realise what you are trying to say you will have to be firmer and actually ask for the talking to stop.

Someone who tries too hard to contribute to the meeting is more difficult to handle. Often they are doing their best and genuinely think that everyone is interested in what they have to say. The only option open to you is to allow them to speak for a reasonable length of time and then say something like: 'So Sarah, you think we should go for the new cars this year. How about you, Roger, what do you think?' This will steer the conversation over to someone else.

THE BIRD-BRAIN

This is the person who seems to have no grey matter at all lurking between the ears. 'Thick' would be another way to describe them. They can hold up the proceedings at a meeting because they have to keep asking questions in order to understand what is being said.

Action to take

The only course of action open to you is to summarise each point that is made in very simple terms, so that **the bird-brain** will understand. If there is still a problem, suggest that they come to see you at the end of the meeting for further explanations. This will stop everyone else becoming exasperated at the lack of progress.

THE EXPERT

We all know someone like this. They are everywhere. At a meeting they are the people that make everyone else groan whenever they open their mouths to speak. **The expert** can talk on any subject at great length. Often they do not know what they are talking about, but just occasionally they do, so they cannot really be silenced until it is too late.

Action to take

Assuming that they are not actually being helpful to the meeting, they should be treated the same as the chatterbox. Try your best to interrupt at a suitable time, thank them for their valuable comments and sharply move the conversation across to someone else.

THE ATTENTION-SEEKER

Most of us know someone we could term an 'attention-seeker' too. **The attention-seeker** needs to feel wanted and listened to. They will often say quite outrageous things just to be noticed.

Action to take

The attention-seeker needs to be indulged – up to a point. Usually such a person is insecure and often quite lonely, so you should start off feeling sorry for them. Try to make them feel involved in the meeting. If possible give them an important job to do – taking notes of the meeting, making the tea – anything so long as they feel useful.

THE PLOTTER

The plotter is someone who intends to wreck the meeting by either blocking or pushing through a particular item. They are often working to a 'hidden agenda', that is, with their fellow plotters they have organised a conspiracy.

Action to take

Try to draw out the plotter by exposing them. For instance, if they are blocking say something like: 'I don't understand why you are so against the new staff rota, Jane. Could you explain your reasons to us?' Once the reasons have been explained, throw the matter open to everyone else.

Someone trying to push an item through needs to be challenged and, if necessary, halted, again calling on everyone else for backing.

Of course, in both instances it is just possible that everyone will agree with the plotter, in which case you will probably be forced to bow to their better judgement!

THE JOKER

Meetings need humour otherwise they become very stuffy affairs. There is, however, a difference between having a good sense of humour and acting the fool. **The joker** will, given the chance, reduce the entire meeting to a joke and nothing at all will be achieved.

Action to take

First of all make sure that you are not overreacting. Humour in small doses will certainly help the meeting along. If you do feel that the humour is being overdone, then speak to the person concerned in a polite way, saying that it is important to keep to the point in order to get through the proceedings.

THE AGGRESSOR

The aggressor is the person who makes rude remarks or personal comments about other people at the meeting. For instance, 'for goodness sake Rachel, what possessed you even to think we could open another store this year? Are you thick or something?'

Action to take

This kind of situation can very quickly get out of hand so stop it straight away. Address the aggressor, letting them see that you will not tolerate such behaviour. 'John, Rachel has done a lot of research into all this. You might not agree with what she says but can we please discuss the matter without including personal remarks?' By retaliating firmly before Rachel gets a chance to say anything, you should defuse the situation. If not, you might need to take the aggressor outside and explain the appropriate language for meetings.

THE WHINGER

The whinger is the person at a meeting who continually finds fault with everyone and everything. Some people seem to like moaning just for the sake of it, even to the point that they are actually unhappy if there is nothing to moan about. Whinging at a meeting can be a real 'downer' for the other participants who just want to get through the proceedings as speedily and successfully as possible.

Action to take

Challenge the whinger. Ask them why they are moaning. Explain that the matters under discussion need to be resolved and if the meeting is to reach a satisfactory conclusion all comments must be restricted to achieving this aim.

THE INTERRUPTER

The interrupter, as their name suggests, interrupts other people whilst they are speaking. This may be because they disagree with what is being said, or because they think their comments would add to the conversation.

Action to take

Unless the interruption is valid, speak firmly to the interrupter saying something like: 'Perhaps you could tell us your views once Rosemary has finished, Peter. If we give her the chance to continue she might resolve the problem for us.' This should give the interrupter the message.

THE SMOKER

Smoking is a very contentious issue everywhere nowadays. Because of the health risks from passive smoking, many people think it is no longer socially acceptable for smoking to take place in public places. The **considerate smoker** will be aware of public feeling and will not smoke in the meeting. The **inconsiderate smoker** will not care about other people and that is when a problem arises.

Action to take

First of all check with the other participants to see if anyone minds the smoker puffing away during the meeting. Usually at least one person will, in which case you will have to explain to the smoker that in everyone's interest you are not permitting smoking in the meeting room. You could offer a break half-way through the meeting so that anyone who is desperate can go out for a quick 'puff'.

CASE STUDIES

Martin feels threatened

Although Martin has turned over a new leaf in an effort to curb his attitude problem, he cannot stand any competition. One thing that he prides himself on is his funny jokes, which unfortunately no one else finds funny. One of the newer reps, Chris, has a brilliant sense of humour and when all the reps go out together for a drink after the meetings he has them all laughing uncontrollably. Martin can cope with this – he only goes with them to the pub occasionally anyway – but when Chris begins lightening up the meetings with his wit, and everyone laughs at him, Martin feels threatened. He decides, therefore, that it is time for a quiet word. He explains to Chris that if there is any humour to be injected into the meeting, he as sales manager, will oblige, but that on the whole everyone's minds must be kept on the business under discussion. Chris smiles to himself as he realises that jealousy is involved here, but he agrees to behave himself in future. Martin compliments himself on his handling of the situation.

George deals with a latecomer

George has a nephew, Andy, who has inherited shares in the business from his father. At 25, Andy is a city whiz-kid, complete with Filofax, mobile phone and flashy car. This does not go down too well with George and his country ways. Andy manages to turn up late for every meeting, breezing in with his phone in one hand and his posh briefcase in the other, waving his hand at everyone and explaining that his late arrival is due to business pressures. On the first two occasions that this happens George goes over the matters discussed so far, giving Andy the benefit of the doubt. When it continues to happen, however, he takes Andy on one side and speaks to him, explaining that unless he can arrive on time, he will not be made welcome at the meetings. No one else likes Andy anyway so they happily back George. Andy, realising that he has got to conform if he is ever to be accepted, makes an effort to be on time in the future.

Sarah deals with a 'no smoking' lobby

The senior doctor in the practice, Dr Jones, smokes and at all the meetings so far everyone has put up with him smoking all the way through, even though behind his back they have objected strongly. Matters come to a head when a new doctor joins the practice and he flatly refuses to attend the meetings if Dr Jones is going to smoke during them. Sarah decides to put the smoking issue on the agenda of one of the practice meetings, asking whether a total ban should be imposed on anyone smoking in the health centre building. When the vote is taken, all the members present go for a total ban, apart from Dr Jones. Realising that he is setting a bad example by smoking at the centre anyway, Dr Jones agrees to go with the majority and a total ban is imposed forthwith.

Anna uses tact

One of the drama club members, Rosemary, is becoming an increasing problem to Anna. At the meetings held during their latest production of *Oliver* she insists on criticising other people's performances, saying that she finds it very difficult to play her own part when everyone else lets her down by their bad acting. In the end the situation gets so bad that Anna asks to see Rosemary on her own. She explain that all the cast do their best and adds tactfully that perhaps Rosemary ought to concentrate on perfecting her own performance, rather than finding fault with other people. At first Rosemary gets very 'huffy', flouncing about the stage, complaining bitterly, but once she realises she is getting no sympathy from anyone, she gets on with improving her acting. As a result the production generally begins to show more promise.

CHECKLIST

Can you cope with: *Method*

- The latecomer ....

- The early leaver ....

- The chatterbox ....

- The bird-brain ....

- The expert ....

- The attention-seeker ....

- The plotter ....

- The joker ....

- The aggressor ....

- The whinger ....

- The interrupter ....

- The smoker? ....

DISCUSSION POINTS

1. What would you do if someone at your meeting found it very difficult to grasp what was being said?

2. How would you handle a person who continually interrupted other people, but usually with valid points?

3. Can you think of some ways to include a very shy participant in the matters being discussed at your meeting?

8
Preparing for the Meeting

WORKING OUT THE AIMS

We talked in the first half of this book about why meetings are held, and presumably by the time you have got as far as preparing for your meeting you will know its main aims or objectives. It is very important that you let everyone attending your meeting know what is to be discussed too, so that they can prepare themselves in advance. We will look at notifying other people in more detail in Chapter 9.

Having worked out your basic aims, the next decision to make is whether you intend to decide everything at one meeting or if you think this is an unrealistic goal. After all, some of the topics might require research after the first meeting before a final decision can be made, or other people may need to be consulted who are not at the meeting. If you think that follow-up meetings are going to be necessary, then you should consider when and where these will be held.

DECIDING ON THE SIZE

The participants at meetings can number anything from two to infinity. For instance, annual general meetings may have several hundred participants, whereas small monthly meetings may have just three or four. The **number of participants** at a meeting will largely be determined by protocol, *ie*, certain people may be entitled to attend if they are directors, shareholders, committee members *etc*. Otherwise it is up to you to invite those people who are directly involved with the matters being discussed and will make a significant contribution to the meeting by their presence.

There are advantages and disadvantages to consider with both small and large meetings.

Small meetings

Advantages
- People are more likely to attend, because they will be noticed if they do not.

- Usually at small meetings everyone knows each other and this makes for confident discussion.

- With most small meetings informality results in higher productivity.

- No one can blend into the background.

Disadvantages
- There may not be the same amount of expertise on a wide range of matters.

- Small meetings can be an excuse for a general 'chit-chat'.

Large meetings

Advantages
- There will be a greater influx of ideas and expertise because of the larger numbers.

- It is easier to control 'wayward' participants due to the more formal atmosphere at most larger meetings.

Disadvantages
- Greater control is needed in order to keep the meeting running smoothly.

- There is more opportunity for the quiet or unresponsive participants to remain silent.

- Often people start to talk amongst themselves, thinking that they will not be noticed in a larger crowd.

- There are more likely to be absentees, as they are less likely to be missed.

To sum up, normally the smaller the meeting the more business is carried out and meetings with between five and ten participants probably stand the best chance of success.

CHOOSING THE VENUE

A meeting can take place almost anywhere – in a corridor, on the bus or train, or even in the car park! Most meetings, however, take place either in a room on the company premises, or in a hotel, hall, or some other outside establishment.

When a meeting is held on the spur of the moment it is not always realistic to think about where to hold it, and this can sometimes be a big mistake. A meeting held in the wrong environment can fail even before it starts if the participants feel uncomfortable for some reason, so whenever possible, give time and care to choosing the venue for your meeting. The main points to think about are:

- The location of the meeting place, in terms of **accessibility** to all the participants.

- The location in relation to **noise and interruptions**. A meeting held next to a busy building site will stand less chance of success than one held in a quiet room where people can concentrate.

- Whether the room is of a suitable **size and shape**. Five people in a massive room will feel remote and inhibited. Similarly 50 people in a room the size of a small family kitchen will make everyone feel claustrophobic and take away their 'space' and security.

- Whether there is access to **equipment** such as computers, fax machines, *etc.*

- Whether there are adequate **power points** to accommodate any visual aids.

- Whether the room is **well lit** and well decorated to encourage positive thinking.

- Whether there are suitable **tables and chairs**.

- In the case of outside accommodation the **cost** of the room or hall will also need to be considered.

Although it is often dismissed as irrelevant, the choice of venue can be a vital factor in the success or failure of the meeting which is to follow.

ARRANGING THE ROOM

Assuming that you have found the ideal room or hall, the next problem to solve is how to arrange the room for maximum effect.

Tables and chairs can be arranged in very many different ways. Some of these are demonstrated on the next two pages. Generally speaking, a large formal meeting will normally benefit from the **theatre** or **classroom** style layout, with rows of chairs, with or without tables, and a desk at the front for the chairperson. Medium-sized meetings may adopt the **boardroom** setting, with a long rectangular table, chairs down both sides, and the chairperson at one end. Small meetings often centre around a circular or small rectangular table, although some small meetings are held very informally with comfortable chairs and no table at all.

Sitting comfortably

A great deal of consideration is given nowadays to the comfort of chairs. Meetings can drag on for a long time and if people are sitting on hard or uncomfortable chairs, their concentration will wander and they will begin to feel restless. The chairs for your meeting should therefore be comfortable and offer good support for the back.

If you are expecting the participants at your meeting to take notes, you will need to provide them with a table and writing materials. Do not assume they will bring their own pens and paper, because many will not.

Everyone at your meeting needs to be able to see and hear, so do not choose a seating arrangement that prevents this. After all, if participants cannot see or hear what is going on they cannot be expected to participate.

Concerning the electrics

Check the lighting and make sure it is adequate for your needs. Look to see where the power points are, particularly if you are intending to use visual aids (see below), and try out the microphone

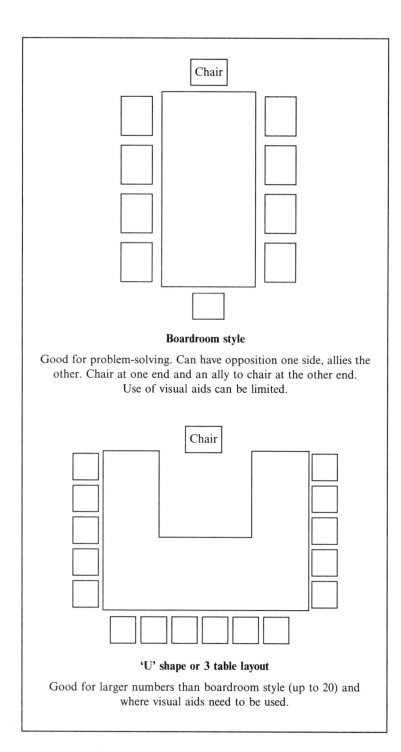

Boardroom style

Good for problem-solving. Can have opposition one side, allies the other. Chair at one end and an ally to chair at the other end. Use of visual aids can be limited.

'U' shape or 3 table layout

Good for larger numbers than boardroom style (up to 20) and where visual aids need to be used.

Fig. 4. Suggested room layouts for a meeting.

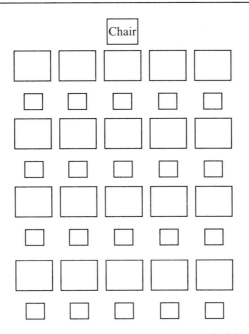

Classroom style (theatre style same but no desks)

Both good for large meetings and conferences, and where visual aids are important.

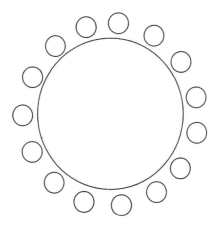

Circular style

Good for brainstorming and to make everyone feel equal.

and any other equipment, just to make sure it is in good working order. Make sure you know where the light switches are too. In a strange hall or hotel room their location might not be obvious and this could cause embarrassment at the time of the meeting.

Doing a final check

All the above should be checked out well in advance of the meeting day. On the day itself, everything should be double-checked, firstly in case you have missed anything, and secondly because certain aspects of the room might have changed since you last looked, *eg*, the types of tables and chairs, the position of the microphone, noisy builders moving into the next room, *etc.*

USING VISUAL AIDS

In order to assist your presentation of certain topics at a meeting it is sometimes advantageous to make use of visual aids. We often take more in through our eyes than through our ears, and so long as the visual aids are used as an *addition* to your verbal presentation, they can work very well.

Examining the different visual aids

There are many different types of visual aids. These include:

Whiteboards
Whiteboards can be a useful way of showing previously prepared information to participants at a meeting or of noting down points made as the meeting progresses. Most of them are, however, of a modest size, so you will need to keep your writing just large enough to see easily, but also small enough to accommodate a reasonable amount of information. Make sure your writing is legible too – whiteboards are not the easiest surface to write on, so get some practice in beforehand.

They are usually fixed to the wall, which means that if everyone is to see what is going on the positioning of tables and chairs is particularly important. It is also important for you to stand to one side of the whiteboard when you are writing on it, so that you are not in anyone's line of vision.

Before using a whiteboard ensure that you have the correct marker pens and that they actually write. Whiteboard pens are notorious for their unreliability at crucial times!

Flip charts

Flip charts have the same uses as whiteboards, but they are normally portable (often supported on a traditional easel) and much more information can be written on them. They can be prepared before the meeting takes place or they can be left blank for notes to be made as the meeting progresses. Your writing will need to be legible, but you will find legible writing easier to achieve on a flip chart than a whiteboard.

If you are going to be using your flip chart a lot during the meeting, it is a good idea to turn up the bottom right hand corner of each page a fraction to facilitate easier flipping over.

Slide projector with slides

Slides can be very effective at a meeting. They add colour and interest and they show detail particularly well. It is very important to check that the slides are inserted the right way and in the correct order, otherwise your audience might be laughing and participating, but not in the way you expected! Most of us have enjoyed a disastrous slide-show at one time or another in the past, much to the acute embarrassment of the person showing the slides. Slides normally need to be shown with the lights dimmed, which can be a good opportunity for everyone to drop off to sleep, so it is up to you to hold the participants' interest by accompanying the slides with interesting commentary.

Overhead projector

An overhead projector uses transparencies which can be prepared either by yourself or professionally. They are easier and less expensive to prepare than slides. The secret is to keep the information simple and to use a good screen in order to achieve the maximum effect. There is normally no need to black out the room, which is a definite advantage over using slides.

Video recorder with television screen

Video recordings are particularly useful when used for training purposes. Professionally prepared ones are best, although amateur videos can be used to illustrate specific business-related points that would not be available professionally.

Handouts

Handouts have become increasingly popular in recent years. They provide a permanent record and they can be used to show a good deal of complicated information that could not be explained effectively at a meeting. There are three main choices of when to give out the handouts:

- before the meeting begins
- during the meeting
- at the end of the meeting.

The type of meeting will dictate which option to choose. For instance, although reading a handout can distract participants from the meeting itself, the information may be relevant to the items being discussed. On the other hand, the handout might explain something that can be read about at any time.

A checklist for visual aids
Whenever you are using any form of visual aid:

- Check to see that everything is working before the meeting.

- Make sure the participants will be able to see and hear.

- Keep the material simple and interesting.

- If you need to turn out the lights check that you will still be able to see any relevant notes.

- Do not turn your back on the audience.

- Have a contingency plan in operation in case the equipment goes wrong, *ie*, transfer to a flip chart, change the order of the meeting *etc*.

Finally remember:

- The visual aids are there to *aid* not to take over the entire meeting for you. Use them *sparingly*.

ORGANISING HOSPITALITY

The amount and type of hospitality you provide for your meeting will depend on the type of meeting, the time of day and the number of resources available.

If your meeting is to be held in a hotel, then the hotel catering staff will prepare whatever you order in the way of refreshments and all you will have to do is pay them afterwards! On the other hand, if the meeting is being held at work, or at your club or organisation, then it will often be down to you to arrange everything yourself.

As an absolute minimum, **water jugs** and **glasses** should always be provided. Most people will also appreciate a short break with tea, coffee and biscuits served either in the room or elsewhere. Alcohol is not to be recommended, at least until the end of the meeting, otherwise judgements may become clouded!

When the meeting stretches over a meal-time, arrange some sandwiches or other **light refreshments**. Once your participants get hungry they will find it hard to concentrate, and begin to feel irritable. It is therefore in everyone's best interests to keep the energy levels up!

Remember above all that happy, well-fed and well-watered people make for a productive meeting and a positive outcome.

CASE STUDIES

Martin rethinks his meeting venue

Martin has always used a conference room at the London head office for his monthly sales meetings. His sales-force covers the whole of the south of England, however, and with increasing amounts of traffic, the sales reps are finding it hard to come into central London so often.

As he is allowed a certain amount of business expenses each month, Martin decides to use some of this to pay for a hotel room for the meetings. He chooses two hotels, one in the east of the region and one in the west, to use on alternate months. He feels that this will mean fewer trips to head office for the reps.

At the same time, Martin rethinks the set-up for his meetings. Up until now he has seated everyone around a conference table with himself at the head. Now he decides to go for a more informal setting – easy chairs and occasional tables – in order to make the reps feel more equal and less inhibited.

George makes use of visual aids

As an 'extra' to one of the regular meetings, George brings in a video machine and specially prepared video which he has received from one of the leading boating agencies. The video gives an insight into how the industry as a whole has changed over the last five years, and makes suggestions on how the boatyards can adapt to their changing future.

The video is shown at the end of the meeting and whilst it is running George arranges for refreshments to be served, so that everyone has something to 'munch' while they watch. This puts the shareholders in a good mood for the informal discussion which follows.

Sarah provides handouts

A meeting is to be held to discuss the proposed acquisition of a nearby house to increase the size of the health centre. Before the meeting takes place Sarah prepares a handout for everyone to read. This outlines the proposals and also includes the estate agent's details of the property to be purchased.

By circulating this in advance everyone has the opportunity to think carefully about their feelings on the matter beforehand.

Anna organises refreshments

Anna has noticed that several members have looked very tired and acted in a very irritable manner at the drama club's last few evening meetings. When she asks them what the problem is they explain that they come straight from work and are feeling quite hungry and weary by the time they arrive.

Anna asks everyone if they would be prepared to contribute £1 each so that she can provide some refreshments at each evening meeting. There is unanimous approval for this idea which is consequently put into immediate effect.

CHECKLIST

- Have you a clear idea of the aims and objectives of the meeting?

- Do the people attending know these too?

- Do you hope to reach a decision on every topic discussed at the meeting?

- Are you inviting the right people to the meeting?

- Have you given consideration to a suitable venue?

- Do you know the best arrangement of furniture for your type of meeting?

- Are the chairs comfortable enough to sit on for some time?

- Is the room or hall heated to an adequate temperature?

- Can you gain access to computer equipment *etc*?

- Are there ample power points, if needed?

- Are you intending to use visual aids?

- If so, have you made the necessary advance preparations?

- Have you thought about refreshments?

- Are you sure that you are providing adequate food and drink for the length of the meeting?

- Can you say to yourself that you have thought about every practical aspect for the smooth running of your meeting?

DISCUSSION POINTS

1. How much do you think the choice of venue affects the success of a meeting?

2. Can you think of visual aids you could use at your meeting that do not require a supply of electricity?

3. When would it be unrealistic to expect a final decision to be made on a particular topic at a meeting?

9
Organising the Paperwork

WORKING WITH A SECRETARY

Meetings almost always generate a considerable amount of paperwork. Where informal meetings are concerned you may be happy to deal with this paperwork on your own. Formal meetings are more complicated, however, and the services of a secretary could be of tremendous benefit to you.

The secretary for your meeting may be:

- your own office personal secretary taking on an additional role

- someone who is not a secretary in the traditional sense of the word, but who has been appointed purely for the purposes of the meeting.

When you are the chairperson for a meeting, it is worth your while building up a good relationship with the secretary. Never be afraid to **delegate**. He or she is there to help rather than hinder and if you can work together as a team your meeting stands a far greater chance of running smoothly.

A good secretary will help you with the advance practical preparations such as the hiring of the room, assist in the preparation of the agenda, take notes as the meeting progresses, and then type up those notes afterwards.

If you are involved in appointing your own secretary, some points to look out for are:

- an ability to cope under pressure

- a sense of humour

- an organised mind

- a friendly and appealing personality

- an ability to listen well to other people

- if possible – proficient shorthand and keyboard skills.

GATHERING INFORMATION

It goes without saying that all relevant information for your meeting should be acquired well in advance. Either you or your secretary will need to find any documents or papers that are required. You may also have to talk to various people and ask their opinion on certain matters. All your research should be both thorough and accurate. One of the main reasons for the failure of meetings is that the matters being discussed have not been properly researched.

As each separate topic is raised at the meeting, every necessary piece of paper should be immediately to hand, otherwise nothing can be properly discussed, and another meeting will have to be called to discuss exactly the same matters all over again. This is a waste of everyone's time and is the sort of occurrence that gives meetings a bad name.

HOLDING A FORMAL MEETING

Sending out the notice of meeting
Before a formal meeting takes place, the people entitled to attend will need to be informed. For some meetings an official **notice of meeting** is a legal requirement, *eg* for the annual general meetings of companies. This states the date, time and place of the meeting, and if a specific single topic is being discussed then this should be mentioned too.

A separate notice of meeting is also very useful when the meeting is not to be held for some time and busy people have been invited to attend. They can then note the date in their diary to ensure that they will be available. An example of a notice of meeting is shown in Figure 5.

Increasingly nowadays the notice of meeting and agenda are combined together, so that everyone knows first that a meeting is going to be held, and secondly what is to be discussed.

Compiling the agenda
An **agenda** is a programme of what is to be discussed at a meeting. Either it can be sent out after the notice or else the two can be combined. Figures 6 and 7 give suggested layouts.

THE ROSELANE CRICKET CLUB

NOTICE OF MEETING

A meeting of the Roselane Cricket Club will be held at the Lakeside Hotel, Granby, on Saturday 5 May 19XX between 1800 hrs and 1930 hrs, to discuss the proposed new pavilion. The Agenda will be circulated at a later date.

J Smith (Miss)
Secretary)

Fig. 5. Notice of meeting.

THE ROSELANE CRICKET CLUB

Meeting of the above organisation at The Lakeside Hotel, Granby, on Saturday 5 May 19XX between 1800 hrs and 1930 hrs, to discuss the proposed new pavilion. (Notice already circulated).

AGENDA

1. Apologies for absence

2. Minutes of the last meeting

3. Matters arising from Minutes

4. Proposed new pavilion and the objections received from nearby neighbours

5   Architect's plans to discuss

6. Fund-raising for the new project

7. Any other business

8. Date of next meeting

J Smith (Miss)
Secretary

Fig. 6. An agenda.

THE ROSELANE CRICKET CLUB

A Meeting of the Roselane Cricket Club will be held at the Lakeside Hotel, Granby, on Saturday 5 May 19XX between 1800 hrs and 1930 hrs, to discuss the proposed new pavilion. The Agenda for the Meeting is given below.

AGENDA

1. Apologies for absence

2. Minutes of last meeting

3. Matters arising from Minutes

4. Proposed new pavilion and the objections received from nearby neighbours

5. Architect's plans to discuss

6. Fund-raising for the new project

7. Any other business

8. Date of next meeting

J Smith (Miss)
Secretary

Fig. 7. Combined notice and agenda.

The headings on a formal agenda follow a fairly standard format. The headings for the Roselane Cricket Club are explained below:

1.   Apologies for absence – giving the names of those people who were invited but could not attend.

2.   Minutes of last meeting – these are usually signed by the chairperson and accepted as a correct record of the proceedings of the last meeting. If the meeting is a 'one off' this heading will not apply.

3.   Matters arising from Minutes – this is a chance to discuss any matters that need further clarification following the last meeting.

4–6. Specific headings for each topic to be discussed.

7.   Any other business – there is a feeling amongst many that this heading should either be dropped altogether, or that only previously arranged items should be discussed, otherwise the meeting can drag on indefinitely.

8.   Date of next meeting – this is usually fixed, at least provisionally, at the end of the meeting.

Any relevant background information should be sent out with the agenda and it is always a good idea to include both a start and finish time for the meeting. A finish time means that not only can the participants plan their day in advance, but also during the meeting you as chairperson will be able to keep an effective rein on the proceedings by using the time framework.

Sometimes a special agenda is prepared for the chairperson. This gives space for notes to be written as the meeting progresses. An example of this is shown in Figure 8.

Always aim to make your agenda as informative as you possibly can. After all, you want people to be keen to come to your meeting and they will only feel keen if the agenda seems worth while. If your agenda causes a big 'yawn' when it is received, what chance does your meeting stand?

Producing the minutes

At a formal meeting it is normally the secretary who will be

THE ROSELANE CRICKET CLUB

Meeting of the above organisation at the Lakeside Hotel, Granby, on Saturday 5 May 19XX between 1800 hrs and 1830 hrs, to discuss the proposed new pavilion. (Notice already circulated).

CHAIRPERSON'S AGENDA

1. Apologies for absence   1

2. Minutes of last meeting   2

3. Matters arising from Minutes   3

4. Proposed new pavilion and   4
   the objections received
   from nearby neighbours

5. Architect's plans to discuss   5

6. Fund-raising for the new project 6

7. Any other business   7

8. Date of next meeting   8

J Smith (Miss)
Secretary

Fig. 8. A chairperson's agenda.

responsible for taking notes on what is said as the meeting proceeds. These notes are not meant to be verbatim (word for word), but they should give an accurate record of what is discussed.

After the meeting, the secretary will type up the notes into draft form for the chairperson to have a look at, before they are finally prepared as **minutes**. It is up to you as chairperson to amend this rough draft as appropriate. Always remember, however, that these minutes should be an accurate record of what went on at the meeting, not what you would have liked to happen.

The final copy of the minutes should follow the same format as the agenda, even if the items are discussed in a different order. They

THE ROSELANE CRICKET CLUB

Minutes of the meeting of the Roselane Cricket Club held at the Lakeside Hotel, Granby, on Saturday 5 May 19XX between 1800 hrs and 1930 hrs, to discuss the proposed new pavilion.

Present:

Martin James (Chairman)
Suzanne Payne (Secretary)
Jane Walsh
David Mann
Andrew Wallis

Minute			Action
13/6	APOLOGIES FOR ABSENCE	Apologies were received from Stuart Lee and Andy Ward.	
13/7	MINUTES OF LAST MEETING	The Minutes of the last Meeting on 6 April 19XX were read and approved as a correct record.	
13/8	MATTERS ARISING FROM MINUTES	There were no matters arising from the previous Minutes.	
13/9	PROPOSED NEW PAVILION AND THE OBJECTIONS RECEIVED FROM NEARBY NEIGHBOURS	Although the pavilion had not yet reached the planning stage, word had got round, and many people living nearby had already voiced their disapproval at the site to be used for this. It was agreed that David Mann would arrange an informal meeting with the residents association to discuss their fears.	DM
13/10	ARCHITECT'S PLANS TO DISCUSS	The latest plans from the architect were viewed and approved by everyone.	
13/11	FUND-RAISING FOR THE NEW PROJECT	Various fund-raising suggestions were made. Jane Walsh agreed to arrange a jumble sale.	JW
13/12	ANY OTHER BUSINESS	There was no other business.	
13/13	DATE OF NEXT MEETING	The next meeting was set for 10 June 19XX.	

Fig. 9. Suggested layout for minutes.

are generally displayed using the 'house style' for the company or organisation they represent. One of the reasons for this is because the minutes are often stored in a minute book or special folder where they will follow on from previous minutes, so continuity of display is important.

An 'action' column at the right-hand side of the minutes can be an effective way of reminding people of their responsibilities for action following the meeting. Usually just their initials are placed in the action column.

There are several different ways of setting out minutes. Figure 9 provides one example.

HOLDING AN INFORMAL MEETING

Contacting everyone
Even when your meeting is informal it is obviously still necessary to **contact** everyone who needs to attend in order to confirm that the proposed day and time is suitable.

Instead of sending out formal notification, you can either telephone the people concerned or send them a brief letter. The information you should give is as follows:

- the day, starting time, finishing time, and place of meeting

- the purpose of the meeting

- any special papers or documents you require individuals to bring with them.

Working to an agenda
When just one subject is to be discussed at your meeting, it is not really necessary to prepare a written agenda. On the other hand, when the meeting is being held to discuss several subjects an informal agenda, sent out in advance, will assist everybody.

A suggested informal agenda is shown in Figure 10.

Preparing a summary
When an informal meeting takes place someone should make **notes** on the points discussed, just the same as for a formal meeting. That person might be you as the chairperson, or you might have a secretary to assist you. Otherwise you will need to seek a willing

WALKERS FROZEN FOODS

Sales meeting – To be held on Wednesday 4 July 19XX from 1400 hrs to 1600 hrs in Office 6b.

To attend: All Sales Reps
            Sales Clerks

To discuss:

		Time
1.	Sales figures for June	30 mins
2.	Estimates for first half of year	15 mins
3.	New dessert range	45 mins
4.	Costings for potato products	30 mins

Please let me know by Monday if you have any further items you wish to discuss, so that the time schedule can be rearranged as necessary.

John Smythe
Sales Manager

30 June 19XX

Fig. 10. An informal agenda.

volunteer! Even when the meeting is little more than a 'chat', one person might remember quite different things to another, so a written record is always a good idea.

After the meeting a **summary** can be prepared and distributed to everyone who attended the meeting. This will serve as confirmation of any decisions taken and any follow up action needed. A suggested layout for an informal summary is shown in Figure 11.

CASE STUDIES

Martin realises the importance of note-taking

As he has decided to go for more informal meetings, Martin wonders whether he ought to record the proceedings any more. Up until now either his secretary or his wife has taken notes on each of the meetings and typed up formal minutes, although these have never been kept in any particular place, such as a minute book.

Martin tries one meeting without note-taking, but over the next few weeks the reps keep asking him about various points discussed because they have forgotten what was decided. He realises that some form of recorded notes are important after all, even for their routine meetings, so he reinstates his secretary, but asks her to prepare informal notes rather than 'stuffy' minutes. This seems to work well. The notes are read by everyone because they make more interesting reading, and they provide a framework for the reps to work with.

George organises the annual general meeting

George is busy organising the annual general meeting of his shareholders. He does it all properly sending out the notice first and then following this up with the agenda. He displays them as follows:

BAXTERS CRUISERS
Notice of meeting

The annual general meeting of the shareholders of Baxters Cruisers will be held at the Riversend Hall on Saturday 15 September 19XX from 1300 hrs to 1600 hrs. The agenda will be circulated at a later date.

George Baxter
Chairman

WALKERS FROZEN FOODS

Notes on Sales Meeting – held on Wednesday 4 July 19XX from 1400 hrs to 1600 hrs in Office 6b.

Item	Outcome	Action
1.	Sales figures for June were shown to be 10% higher than for the previous month.	
2.	Estimates for the first half of the year were expected to show a significant rise over the last six months of 19XX. According to John this was largely because of the increased demand for frozen desserts.	
3.	The new dessert range was discussed at length. Everyone agreed that sales were up, particularly for the chocolate meringues and the low calorie cheesecake. Bob Williams said he would speak to the research department to see if a new range of Christmas specialities could be introduced in November.	Bob Williams
4.	The cost of potatoes continued to rise. After much discussion it was decided to hold prices for a further month. Connors had already increased the price of their chips so if Walkers could take some of their trade this might offset a price rise. Alison Pye agreed to get a current Connors' price list.	Alison Pye

Next Meeting will be held on Wednesday 3 August. Same time, same place. Agenda to follow.

Fig. 11. An informal summary.

BAXTERS CRUISERS

Annual General Meeting of the shareholders of Baxters Cruisers, at Riversend Hall on Saturday 15 September 19XX from 1300 hrs to 1600 hrs. (Notice already circulated.)

Agenda *Minute*
135.1   Apologies for absence
135.2   Minutes of the last meeting
135.3   Matters arising out of the minutes
135.4   Proposed new cruisers for next season
135.5   Refurbishment of ten existing cruisers
135.6   Continued difficult trading conditions
135.7   Prospects for the next five years
135.8   Any other business (to be notified to the Chairman in advance of the meeting)
135.9   Date of next meeting

George Baxter
Chairman

Sarah sends written notification

Sarah has organised a second meeting to discuss the buying of a nearby house to incorporate into the health centre. Since fixing the meeting two of the doctors have booked holiday leave, saying that they had forgotten all about it. Rather than arrange the meeting time orally as she did before, Sarah sends out a note to everyone explaining the situation and giving an alternative date and time. She asks for immediate notification if anyone is not able to make this new date. By putting the details in writing everyone takes it more seriously and she gets a full attendance as a result.

Anna is pleased with her new secretary

Anna has a new secretary on the committee who is super-efficient. Her previous secretary actually worked as a builder, so his shorthand and typing skills were not up to much, but the new person works at a keyboard all day and she knows how to set things out properly.

Although Anna goes through a period of feeling threatened by this lady's efficiency, she soon realises that well displayed, typed minutes are a lot more help than the scrawled notes she has been receiving so far. Marjorie, the new lady, even manages to produce a minute book so that the minutes can be filed in order and referred to whenever necessary.

CHECKLIST

- Do you have a secretary to help you with meetings?

- If so, do the two of you work as a team?

- Have you obtained all the necessary information for your meeting?

- Are you aware of how to set out the documents used at formal meetings?

- Do you know the purpose of the various headings on the agenda and minutes?

- Can you produce relevant paperwork for an informal meeting?

DISCUSSION POINTS

1. What do you see as the advantages and disadvantages of formal meetings?

2. Can an informal meeting be sufficiently disciplined?

3. Do you think a time limit should be enforced at meetings?

10
Chairing the Meeting

DECIDING WHETHER TO HAVE A 'CHAIR'

Theoretically speaking, in a democratic society, we ought to be able to sit around a table and hold our meetings as an equal team working together to generate ideas, solve problems and make decisions without anybody being in charge. Indeed many meetings do work in this way, especially brainstorming sessions.

Formal meetings, such as annual general meetings of limited companies, are required by law to have a **chairperson** presiding. The vast majority of other meetings also operate with a chairperson. The main reason for this is that meetings involve groups of people and in general groups operate more effectively with a leader.

An effective chairperson will show authority whilst allowing all the participants to express their views. An effective chairperson will keep to a strict time schedule and prevent someone from rambling on and on, but most importantly of all, an effective chairperson will ensure that by the end of the meeting all the objectives have been achieved.

ARRIVING AT THE RIGHT TIME

Try to arrive at the meeting ten to 15 minutes early. As soon as you get there make sure that:

- there are no noise problems to disturb the meeting

- the furniture is arranged in the correct way

- there are pads and pens *etc*

- water jugs and glasses are available.

It is always a good idea to carry extra copies of the agenda and any additional documents that have been sent out in advance, in case anyone forgets to bring their copy.

As the participants arrive, greet them individually. Name plates can be a help for large meetings, but otherwise show each person the seat you have reserved for them. A few friendly words can help to break the ice, although it is best not to start a complicated conversation with someone, otherwise you might not be available to greet other people as they come in.

Finally, take a few deep breaths to calm your nerves so that you are feeling in control and ready to begin the meeting.

OPENING THE MEETING

The moment has finally arrived. All eyes are on you as you rise to declare the meeting open. A few more deep breaths, a look at the clock to check the time, and the meeting is in session.

Never wait for late arrivals. It is most important that you establish your authority and set the ground rules right at the beginning. You need to show that you are in charge, but on the other hand you do not want to appear either bossy or dictatorial. Quietly confident sums up the image you should portray.

Making introductions

First, introduce yourself if everyone does not know who you are. Secondly, introduce any new participants to the meeting, so that they do not feel awkward and left out. Be very careful to get other people's names right. Introducing someone by the wrong name rather undermines your good intentions! Thank everyone for coming. They may not have had much option, but it is still common courtesy.

Getting under way

Having dealt with the 'niceties', go on to state the purpose of the meeting. Run through the agenda and make sure that all the items are still relevant. Ask whether anyone has a particularly urgent matter that should be added to any other business. If there is an addition you might have to miss off one of the non-urgent any other business items, or else extend the meeting by an agreed amount of time.

Once the agenda is agreed, and any other formalities, such as apologies for absence, are out of the way, introduce the first item to be discussed. Depending on the subject, you can either open the discussion yourself or hand over to someone else who happens to be dealing with that particular matter. Once you reach that stage, the meeting is well under way.

CONTROLLING THE MEETING

Never lose sight of the fact that you are in charge of the meeting. It is up to you to steer everyone slowly but surely forwards, keeping to the agenda at all times. Introduce each item, say why it is being discussed, and encourage all the participants to speak, one by one. Make sure that everyone gets a chance to talk, not just a privileged few.

Take time out to clarify any issues that seem to be causing confusion and as each item is finished with, summarise what has been said, so that everyone can 're-cap'.

Keep a close eye on the time and if you feel a particular item is dragging on too long, try to bring the discussion to a close, politely but firmly.

Giving praise where praise is due will help the meeting along too. Everyone likes to feel appreciated and if a participant has been particularly helpful then say so.

Knowing your group

An understanding of people and what makes them tick will help you chair your meeting in the best way possible. We have already talked about group behaviour, and it is very important for you to understand specifically the group of people you have at your meeting, and how they interact with one another. It is also important for them to understand you, and to feel that you are there to give positive backing rather than to find fault with what they say.

HANDLING THE HIDDEN AGENDA

The term **hidden agenda** in the context of meetings means issues other than those listed on the agenda that are raised by one or more participants.

The hidden agenda does not always have to be destructive. A participant may want to add something positive to the meeting, even though it is not on the agenda. If you feel this to be the case, then you would do well to allow the participant to continue.

Handling conspirators

On the other hand, one or a group of participants could be out to show superiority over you and the other members by trying to wreck the meeting. In these circumstances you have two options, either to ignore the undercurrent and hope it will go away, or to confront it. If you choose the latter, try to embarrass the conspirators by exposing them in front of everyone else and, assuming you are reasonably sure of support, ask your loyal participants to back you.

Always be on the look out for a hidden agenda. By watching other people's body language, the way they are sitting, giggles and whispers, and a sudden alertness when you mention a particular issue, you will soon know when a hidden agenda is in operation. It is up to you to control it!

SUMMARISING THE DISCUSSIONS

By summarising each item as the meeting progresses, everyone will be kept fully informed. At a formal meeting decisions are taken mainly by voting for or against a 'motion' (see Glossary) put forward by one participant and seconded by another. At an informal meeting decisions are usually reached by group discussion, although in some cases votes are still taken, particularly when agreement cannot be reached.

Allow time for everyone to express their views and then try to summarise the arguments for and against. After that give your own views on the matter. Once agreement has been reached, you or your secretary should note this down.

ACHIEVING THE AIMS

By the end of the meeting you should have a clear indication of whether or not all the aims have been achieved. Obviously your aim will be to cover everything, but any matters still unresolved will have to be carried over to the next meeting. Do not be tempted to run the meeting over time. If you do you will upset those participants who have made arrangements on the understanding that the meeting will finish at a certain time.

Managing a meeting is a balancing act between the amount of time available and the number of items to be discussed and resolved. There is also the human element that can never be completely accounted for. Some of your participants will always say ten sentences when two would do, and others will insist on questioning everything that other people say. If you have too many of either of these types, the progress of your meeting will be slowed down considerably. You can try your best to push things along, but you cannot work miracles!

At the end of the day, if you are able to say that you have achieved as many objectives as you could realistically expect from the meeting, then your role as chairperson has been a success.

CASE STUDIES

Martin feels at ease

At the beginning of the book Martin was holding formal monthly sales meetings where he made sure everyone was aware of his superiority by being aggressive and dictatorial. He has gradually realised, however, that his more informal approach and friendly 'chairing' actually produces far better results from his sales team. He has his wife to thank for this, because until she sat in on a meeting, he was really unaware of just what he was doing wrong.

Apart from achieving a higher degree of success with his meetings, Martin has also become a much happier and fulfilled person. He really enjoys his job now, and looks forward to his meetings too.

George congratulates himself

George chairs his annual general meeting with fear and trepidation, but as it turns out everything runs very smoothly. He introduces each item and manages to control the shareholders throughout. He cannot believe how polite everyone is and how they all wait their turn to speak. He keeps to the time schedule and at the end of the meeting he gives himself a big pat on the back. He is not a conceited man but he feels very lucky that he has survived so well!

Sarah copes with 'stirrers'

Sarah finally gets to chair the meeting to discuss the purchase of a nearby house to increase the size of the health centre.

Sarah has to deal with two 'stirrers' who do not really care one way or the other about buying the house, but just want to cause trouble by disagreeing with everyone. The two people in question, both nurses at the centre, have recently fallen out with the doctors over the hours that they work. They know the doctors want to buy the house so, pettily, they don't want them to have it.

In the end Sarah challenges them and asks them why they oppose the idea. Neither of them can come up with a rational answer, rather as Sarah expected. She tells everyone that a vote will be taken and an overwhelming majority (everyone except the two nurses) votes in favour of going ahead.

Sarah explains that in view of the vote the purchase will proceed with all haste, so that work can begin on the conversion as soon as feasibly possible. The two nurses accept that they are beaten, and walk out. Sarah ignores their departure and closes the meeting with the confidence and efficiency she has shown all the way through.

Anna learns how to delegate
At the next annual general meeting, Anna has secretarial help for the first time. Marjorie is very efficient and Anna is able to concentrate on the job in hand, which is primarily to elect new committee members. Her own job as chairman is only changed every three years, so she is not affected personally.

All the new committee members are chosen without any problems with Marjorie being officially voted into the secretary's position. Anna realises that it is actually better to share her duties with someone rather than try to do it all herself. She tells Marjorie that she looks forward to their team effort continuing and the two women become firm friends.

CHECKLIST

- Are you aware of the advantages of having a 'leader' at meetings?

- Do you always arrive a few minutes early for your meetings?

- Do you check to make sure that everything is in order before everyone else arrives?

- Do you greet the participants in a friendly manner as they come in?

- Do you show a quietly confident attitude when opening your meetings?

- Does your opening speech effectively set the scene?

- Are you able to keep control of your meetings?

- Do you remember to summarise each item after discussion?

- Can you cope with a hidden agenda?

- Are you able to sum up effectively at the end of your meetings and ensure that the right decisions are taken?

- Can you say to yourself that you always do your best to make sure your meetings achieve their aims?

DISCUSSION POINTS

1. What instances can you think of when a chairperson would not be appropriate to preside over a meeting?

2. How would you deal with a hidden agenda involving a plot to oust you as chairperson?

3. Do you see the chairperson as the most important person at a meeting?

11
Following-up the Meeting

WAS THE MEETING A SUCCESS?

After your meeting has taken place, perhaps the first question you should ask yourself is whether it was successful. Bad points as well as good can be analysed and used to help plan meetings in the future.

Try asking yourself the following questions:

- Was the meeting held on the **best day** and at the best time to achieve a satisfactory outcome?

- Did it start and finish **on time**?

- Were the **correct people** in attendance?

- Was the **agenda** followed in the correct order?

- Were **accurate notes** taken?

- Were the **right decisions** made?

- Did the meeting **achieve** what it set out to achieve?

The more answers of 'yes' you can give, the better. Any 'no's' need to be investigated, so that future meetings stand a chance of being as near to perfect as anything involving the human element can ever be.

IMPLEMENTING DECISIONS

One of the biggest problems with meetings is that people say they will take action on a specific topic, and then as soon as they leave the meeting they promptly forget all about what they have agreed to do.

Taking accurate notes or minutes will help to eliminate this problem, but not everyone will bother to read the notes, so some 'chivvying' will probably still be necessary.

Getting some action

There is obviously no point in making decisions if they are not going to be acted on, and you should ensure that the appropriate people give a firm commitment and keep to it. After all, the results of a meeting cannot be seen until something has actually been done.

A failure to act on decisions can lower the morale of all the participants, when it is often only one or two of them who are actually at fault. If you are having trouble with people failing in their duties, try to point out tactfully that the success of the meeting rests with them, and that action must be taken promptly in order to achieve the maximum benefits from the decision.

Remember, above all, that it is a complete waste of time holding another related meeting until the appropriate decisions from the first meeting have been implemented.

SENDING CORRESPONDENCE

Whether formal minutes or informal notes have been taken at your meeting, it is very important to see that the final copies are sent out to the appropriate people as soon as possible. These may be prepared by you or by your secretary.

The minutes or notes can be accompanied by a short **letter or memo**, explaining any specific points, and gently reminding people about their 'action' duties.

Additional correspondence

It may, of course, also be necessary to send out other letters and memos in connection with the meeting. For example, perhaps an outside contractor is going to be asked to quote for an extension to your office, or the personnel department needs to be notified about a new employment campaign. Make these letters or memos as clear and concise as you can. After all, if you cannot explain yourself properly, you cannot expect anyone else to understand what you are asking them to do.

THINKING ABOUT YOUR PERFORMANCE

It is all very well for you to criticise other people for their inadequacies, but what of your own? At the end of any meeting take a look at yourself and your performance. Ask yourself the following:

- Was I **well prepared** for everything I had to deal with?

- Did I show the **right attitude** to the other participants?

- Did I **dominate** the meeting too much?

- Did everyone else get a chance to **put their views** forward?

- Did I **deal effectively** with problem people?

- Did I **dress appropriately**?

- Did I have to deal with any **embarrassing moments**?

If things went well then congratulate yourself and try to pinpoint the specific reasons for the successful outcome. If they went badly, think about how you will be able to put them right another time.

All of us need to continue learning and developing, otherwise we become boring to ourselves and to other people. A 'meetings' situation is no exception to this. We can all learn by our mistakes and build on our successes at meetings just the same as in every other area of our life.

ASKING FOR FEEDBACK

It is a good idea – if you are brave enough – to ask the participants at your meeting what they thought about its effectiveness. After all, other people can often come up with ideas and suggestions for improvement that you had not even thought about.

Feedback from your colleagues can form an important part of your strategy for the future. If you do not like actually asking everyone at the end of the meeting, then try giving them a **questionnaire** to take home. They can then return this to you at their leisure, anonymously if this is thought preferable.

An example of a questionnaire is given in Figure 12.

FOLLOW-UP QUESTIONNAIRE

Did you enjoy the meeting?   Yes/No*

Did you understand the objectives
of the meeting?   Yes/No*

In your opinion, were those objectives
achieved?   Yes/No*

Did you feel you were given enough
opportunity to contribute?   Yes/No*

Were you told about the meeting
early enough?   Yes/No*

Was it arranged at a time to suit
your commitments?   Yes/No*

Was the location a convenient one
for you?   Yes/No*

Have you taken any follow-up action
agreed at the meeting?   Yes/No*

*Please delete as applicable and return to .... as
soon as possible. You do not need to add your name to the
Questionnaire unless you wish to do so.

Fig. 12. A questionnaire to receive feedback after a meeting.

MEETINGS OF THE FUTURE

Following up your meeting, next month or next year, is one thing. But how about the meetings of the rather more distant future? What type of meetings will be held in five or ten years' time for example?

The average drama, sports or social club will probably carry on with their meetings in much the same way for as long as we need to worry about. In the same way, annual general meetings of important shareholders held in prestigious hotels will also probably continue for many years to come.

Most everyday business meetings, however, are office based, and the office of the future is likely to be very different from the office of the present. Already we are seeing a rapid move away from large business organisations in favour of smaller outlets set up throughout the country, using 'networking' by computer link-up. There are also an increasing number of people working from their own homes.

So will the everyday business meeting disappear altogether if this trend continues? The short answer is 'no'. What will probably happen is that the people organising meetings will become more selective, only calling a meeting when it is really necessary, because the participants may be travelling some considerable distance. Because of their isolation though, people will feel the need even more to meet from time to time for an interaction of ideas and policies.

Another probability is that 'video conferencing', where people can link up for a meeting thousands of miles away by means of satellite television, will become very widely used throughout the world.

There's no escape. The meeting is certainly here to stay. But at least you are now fully equipped to tackle all your meetings of the future, whatever form they may take, with confidence and enthusiasm.

CASE STUDIES

Martin shows his appreciation

At the next monthly sales meeting, Martin tells his reps that he intends to take them out for a really good meal at Christmas. He says that partners can come too and that he is going to book one of the best hotels in London for the occasion, with overnight accommodation for everyone. He has been very frugal with his expenses budget over the last few months to pay for some of this, but he intends to take the rest of the money out of his own salary, as a 'thank you' for their greatly improved targets.

Martin knows that he earns more commission if his reps perform well, and he feels they need 'spoiling' for their efforts. As far as 'follow-up' is concerned, he sees this as a very positive way of encouraging everyone to work hard in the future, both out in the field and at their monthly meetings.

George enjoys being part of a team

George is getting used to the business being owned by several people rather than just him. In fact he is rather enjoying his new status, which in a way makes him feel more important than before, when he just had himself to answer to.

After the annual general meeting George writes a letter to every shareholder, which he encloses with a copy of the minutes. He says how much he enjoyed meeting them and the opportunity this presented to discuss the future of Baxters Cruisers. He stresses that he also looks forward to working with them all in the future and that he firmly believes that between them they will make Baxters into the best boating company in the entire country.

George's positive, yet down-to-earth attitude is what is needed to keep all these family members working together, rather than against one another.

Sarah is kept busy

Sarah has a good deal of correspondence to take care of following the recent practice meeting. First, she writes to the estate agents, putting in a formal offer for the house they wish to buy. When she receives formal acceptance of this offer, she writes to each of the doctors outlining what their financial contribution will need to be, and asking for their provisional agreement to the quoted figures. Finally, she writes to their solicitor asking him to act for the practice in the purchase.

The health centre does eventually expand and Sarah finds herself busier than ever. She really enjoys her job, even if the meetings she has to chair are a little stressful at times!

Anna is feeling positive about the future

Anna drafts out a letter to each of the new committee members welcoming them and outlining their duties. Marjorie, her new found 'treasure', types them out and sends them with copies of the minutes.

Anna feels that with Marjorie as 'back-up' their future meetings will be more productive and better prepared. She wants to increase the number of productions they do each year, and feels that this is now the time to do so. Anna finds herself enjoying the drama club more than she has done for years and she even finds time to do some acting herself.

CHECKLIST

- Did the meeting achieve a satisfactory outcome?

- Have the decisions taken at the meeting been implemented?

- Have you or your secretary sent out the minutes or notes of the meeting?

- Have you also dealt with any other correspondence arising from the meeting?

- Do you think you personally performed well at the meeting?

- If you did, what were your specific successes?

- If the meeting went badly, do you know where you went wrong and what you need to do differently next time?

- Have you asked the other participants for their views on the success of the meeting?

- Are you prepared to listen to them?

DISCUSSION POINTS

1. How important do you think effective follow-up to a meeting really is?

2. What do you see as your strengths and weaknesses in connection with chairing a meeting?

3. Do you think it is always important to record permanently what goes on at a meeting and send out a copy to everyone who attended? Give reasons for your answer.

Appendix

NATIONAL VOCATIONAL QUALIFICATIONS LEVELS 1, 2 AND 3

National Vocational Qualifications (NVQs) have been recently introduced by the National Council for Vocational Qualifications. They are available in many different subjects. Those intended to help office workers are Administration Levels 1, 2 and 3. The criteria for these NVQs were revised in 1994 and 1995.

Conventional examinations aim to test your formal skill and knowledge in one or more particular subjects. NVQs are designed to prove that you can put your exam success to good use in the workplace. They deal with the practical aspects of your work.

NVQs are made up of different units. Certificates can be awarded for just one or more units, if you do not want to go on and take the full certificate.

The specific subject of this book, *ie* meetings, is an optional part of both levels 2 and 3. However, many of the other units touch on the subject in a more general way, so the full criteria for both levels is given below.

ADMINISTRATION LEVEL 2

At level 2 there are eight mandatory units and seven optional units. You will only be awarded the NVQ if you achieve all the mandatory units and at least one of the optional units. In addition, if you achieve the full NVQ and then complete extra optional units, these will also be certificated. If you achieve fewer than nine units you will receive a Certificate of Unit Credit for each unit that you do complete.

Mandatory units

Unit 1: Develop self to improve performance
Element 1.1   Identify and agree own development needs
Element 1.2   Prepare and agree a plan of action to develop self
Element 1.3   Implement and review a personal development plan

Unit 2: Monitor and maintain a healthy, safe and secure workplace
Element 2.1   Monitor and maintain health and safety within the workplace
Element 2.2   Monitor and maintain the security of the workplace

Unit 3: Contribute to the effectiveness of the workflow
Element 3.1   Plan and organise own work schedule
Element 3.2   Obtain and organise information in support of own work activities
Element 3.3   Obtain and maintain physical resources to carry out own work

Unit 4: Create and maintain effective working relationships
Element 4.1   Establish and maintain working relationships with other members of staff
Element 4.2   Receive and assist visitors

Unit 5: Store, retrieve and supply information
Element 5.1   Maintain an established storage system
Element 5.2   Supply information for a specific purpose

Unit 6: Maintain data in a computer system
Element 6.1   Input data and text into a computer system
Element 6.2   Locate and retrieve data from a computer system
Element 6.3   Print documents using a computer system

Unit 7: Prepare documents
Element 7.1   Respond to correspondence
Element 7.2   Prepare a variety of documents

Unit 8: Receive and transmit information
Element 8.1   Receive and transmit information electronically
Element 8.2   Receive and send mail

Unit 9: Maintain and issue stock items
Element 9.1   Order, monitor and maintain stock
Element 9.2   Issue stock items on request

Option units

Unit 10: Process documents relating to goods and services
Element 10.1   Order goods and services
Element 10.2   Process claims for payment

Unit 11: Organise travel and accommodation arrangements
Element 11.1   Arrange travel for persons
Element 11.2   Book accommodation for a specified purpose

Unit 12: Contribute to the arrangement of events
Element 12.1   Assist in arrangements for the provision of supporting facilities and materials at events
Element 12.2   Assist in arrangements for the attendance of persons at events
Element 12.3   Assist in arrangements for the provision of catering services at events

Unit 13: Produce and present business documents from provided material
Element 13.1   Produce business documents from provided material using a keyboard
Element 13.2   Present business documents in a variety of formats using a keyboard

Unit 14: Produce and present business documents from recorded material
Element 14.1   Produce business documents from recorded instructions using a keyboard
Element 14.2   Present business documents in a variety of formats using a keyboard

Unit 15: Produce and present business documents from dictated material
Element 15.1 Produce business documents from dictated information using a keyboard
Element 15.2 Present business documents in a variety of formats using a keyboard

ADMINISTRATION LEVEL 3

At level 3 there are eight mandatory units and seven optional units. A certificate will be issued to candidates completing all the mandatory units. Any Option units achieved at the same time will additionally be listed on the certificate. Individual units achieved will be recognised by a Certificate of Unit Credit. Candidates can, if they wish, build these credits up over a period of time to achieve the full award.

Mandatory units

Unit 1: Contribute to the improvement of performance
Element 1.1 Develop self to enhance performance
Element 1.2 Contribute to improving the performance of colleagues

Unit 2: Contribute to the maintenance of a healthy, safe and effective working environment
Element 2.1 Monitor and maintain a safe, healthy and secure workplace
Element 2.2 Maintain effective working conditions

Unit 3: Contribute to the planning, organising and monitoring of work
Element 3.1 Plan and agree work
Element 3.2 Monitor and control the achievement of agreed targets
Element 3.3 Manage appointments

Unit 4: Create, develop and maintain effective working relationships
Element 4.1 Create, develop and maintain effective working relationships with colleagues
Element 4.2 Create, develop and maintain effective working relationships with external contacts

Unit 5: Research, prepare and supply information
Element 5.1   Research, locate and select information to meet specified needs
Element 5.2   Prepare and supply information to meet specified needs

Unit 6: Enter and integrate data, and present information using a computer system
Element 6.1   Enter data into a computer
Element 6.2   Integrate different types of data
Element 6.3   Present information in various formats

Unit 7: Draft and prepare documents
Element 7.1   Draft documents to meet specified requirements
Element 7.2   Initiate and respond to correspondence

Unit 8: Develop, implement and maintain procedures
Element 8.1   Develop procedure to meet specified needs
Element 8.2   Implement and maintain procedures

Option units

Unit 9: Obtain, organise and monitor the use of material and equipment
Element 9.1   Obtain and organise materials and equipment
Element 9.2   Monitor the use of materials and equipment

Unit 10: Organise and record meetings
Element 10.1   Arrange and prepare for meetings
Element 10.2   Attend, support and record meetings
Element 10.3   Produce and progress records of meetings

Unit 11: Arrange and monitor travel and accommodation
Element 11.1   Organise travel and accommodation arrangements
Element 11.2   Monitor and verify travel and accommodation arrangements

Unit 12: Contribute to the acquisition and control of financial provision
Element 12.1   Contribute to the acquisition of financial provision
Element 12.2   Contribute to the control of financial provision

Unit 13: Prepare, produce and present documents using a variety of sources of information
Element 13.1   Research and prepare information
Element 13.2   Produce and present documents using a keyboard

Unit 14: Prepare, produce and present documents from own notes
Element 14.1   Take notes and prepare information
Element 14.2   Produce and present documents using a keyboard

Unit 15: Prepare, produce and present documents from recorded speech
Element 15.1   Prepare information from variable quality recorded speech
Element 15.2   Produce and present documents using a keyboard

Glossary

Abstain. To refrain from voting.

Addendum. To add words.

Address the chair. This means that those wishing to speak must do so by speaking to the person in the chair, *ie* the chairperson, rather than carrying on conversations between themselves.

Ad hoc. This usually refers to a committee specially appointed to carry out a specific task (rather than a permanent or 'standing' committee).

Adjournment. A decision taken to adjourn the meeting.

Agenda. The list of items to be discussed at a meeting.

Amendment. A proposal to alter a 'motion'. It must be proposed, seconded and voted on before a decision is taken.

Any other business. The 'any other business' time in a meeting gives an opportunity for those present to discuss items other than those listed under separate headings. It is often abbreviated to AOB.

Attitude. The way we think or behave.

Ballot. A method of voting by means of a voting paper.

Behaviour. The way in which people behave.

Body language. The way we communicate by using different parts of our body rather than the spoken word.

Brainstorming. A meeting where everyone puts forward their plans to solve a specific problem or to generate new ideas.

Call to order. A call by the chairperson for those present to return to the matter in hand, and if necessary, to begin behaving in a proper manner.

Carried. A motion that has been agreed.

Casting vote. If voting on a motion is equal, the chairperson may have the power to cast his or her vote, thus making the decision.

Chairperson. The person in charge of a meeting.

Committee. A group of people who meet to make decisions on behalf of an organisation.

Communicate. To give, receive, or exchange information.

Consensus. General agreement on a subject.

Constitution. The rules governing the objectives, structure and functions of an organisation.

Deadline. Time limit.

Decision. Course of action decided upon.

Delegate. Someone who represents a group of people and gives their views.

Draft. The first rough copy of a document.

Edit. To check a document for spelling and grammatical errors.

Environment. The surroundings we live and work in.

Evaluate. To review the result of a decision or solution.

Ex officio. A person who is a member of a meeting due to his or her office, but who cannot vote.

In camera. A meeting in private, not open to the public.

Interpret. Explain the meaning of something.

Interview. Formal conversation between two or more people with a specific aim in mind.

In the chair. The person who is in control of the meeting, *ie* the chairperson.

Layout. The way a document is displayed.

Lie on the table. This is when a document is not to be acted on and it is said to 'lie on the table'.

Limited. A popular form of business organisation, owned by its shareholders and managed by its directors. It can be either a private limited company (Ltd after the name), or a public limited company (plc after the name). In a private limited company the owners put money in by buying shares. In a public limited company the shares are sold to the general public, often through the stock exchange.

Majority. This means the number of votes necessary to carry a motion.

Minutes. Notes containing important points of a meeting.

Motion. A proposal put forward at a meeting is known as a motion. When a motion is put forward it is known as a question. If it is passed it is known as a resolution. It is usually necessary to propose and second a motion before it can be discussed.

Motivate. To prompt ourselves or others into action.

Objectives. Targets or goals to be achieved.

Out of order. Not in accordance with the rules.

Point of order. A question put to the chairperson which requires an answer and interrupts the proceedings of the meeting.

Postponement. This is the action taken to put off a meeting to a later date.

Problem. A situation requiring a solution.

Proxy vote. A person who cannot attend a meeting can ask someone else to vote on his or her behalf. The person is known as a proxy and the vote is called a proxy vote.

Quorum. With most formal meetings a certain number of people must be present before the meeting can take place. This number is known as a quorum.

Relevant. Applicable to the subject.

Resolution. A motion passed at a meeting.

Secretary. Person responsible for the administration of a formal meeting.

Show of hands. A method of voting where members raise their hands to indicate their preference.

Team. A group of people working together to achieve specific aims.

Unanimous. All of one mind.

Verbatim. Word for word.

Veto. The power of a person to prevent a proposal being acted upon.

Vote of thanks. A meeting may close with a 'vote of thanks' to show appreciation to the people who have arranged and conducted the meeting.

Waffle. Flowery language which does not come straight to the point.

Further Reading

The Perfect Meeting, David Sharman (Century Business Books, 1992).

Successful Meeings in a Week, John and Shirley Payne (Hodder & Stoughton, 1994).

The Secrets of Successful Business Meetings, Gordon Bell (Heinemann, 1990).

How to Take Minutes of Meetings, Jennie Hawthorne (Kogan Page, 1993).

Secretarial Duties, John Harrison (Pitman, 1992).

Success in Communication, Stuart Sillars (John Murray, 1988).

Collins Office Handbook, Louise Bostock (HarperCollins, 1993).

Debrett's Etiquette and Modern Manners, edited by Elsie Burch Donald (Headline, 1995).

How to Master Public Speaking, Anne Nicholls (How To Books, 1995).

How to Manage People at Work, John Humphries (How To Books, 1995).

How to Communicate at Work, Ann Dobson (How To Books, 1994).

How to Manage an Office, Ann Dobson (How To Books, 1995).

Index

How to Manage Computers at Work
Graham Jones

Here is a practical step-by-step guide which puts the business needs of the user first. It discusses why a computer may be needed, how to choose the right one and instal it properly; how to process letters and documents, manage accounts, and handle customer and other records and mailing lists. It also explains how to use computers for business presentations, and desktop publishing. If you feel you should be using a computer at work, but are not sure how to start, then this is definitely the book for you.. and you won't need an electronics degree to start! 'Bags of information in a lingo we can all understand. I strongly recommend the book.' *Progress/NEBS Management Association*. Graham Jones has long experience of handling personal computers for small business management. The Managing Director of a desktop publishing company, he is also author of *How to Start a Business from Home* and *How to Publish a Newsletter* in this Series.

160pp 1 85703 078 8.

How to Manage Budgets & Cash Flows
Peter Taylor

Today, it is not just accountants and book-keepers who manage budgets and cash flows. Increasingly it is a job for all business managers, whether in private firms or public sector organisations such as hospitals or schools. Written by an experienced chartered accountant, this book provides a basic step-by-step introduction to practical budget and cash flow management. It covers planning, forecasting, budgeting, to monitoring performance, both as to current income, and as to capital expenditure on such things as new premises, plant and equipment. The book also covers VAT, costings and margins, and using computers, plus helpful action checklists and short case studies.

160pp illus. 1 85703 066 4.

How to Work in an Office
Sheila Payne

Thousands of school/college leavers – and mature returners – go to work in offices every year. But what exactly is an office? What functions does it perform? What tasks need to be done? With its clearly written text, examples and short case studies, this helpful book will provide an excellent preparation for everyone entering the world of office work for the first time. Sheila Payne is an office skills trainer; she holds teacher's diplomas in typewriting and word-processing, and the City & Guilds Youth Trainers Award/Vocational Assessors Award.

160pp illus. 1 85703 094 X.

How to Keep Business Accounts
Peter Taylor

The third fully revised edition of an easy-to-understand handbook for all business owners and managers. 'Will help you sort out the best way to carry out double entry book-keeping, as well as providing a clear step-by-step guide to accounting procedures.' *Mind Your Own Business.* 'Progresses through the steps to be taken to maintain an effective double entry book-keeping system with the minimum of bother.' *The Accounting Technician.* 'Compulsory reading.' *Manager, National Westminster Bank (Midlands).* Peter Taylor is a Fellow of the Institute of Chartered Accountants, and of the Chartered Association of Certified Accountants. He has many years' practical experience of advising small businesses.

176pp illus. 1 85703 111 3. Third edition.

How to Counsel People at Work
John Humphries

The value of counselling has become much better recognised in recent times, as a tool for addressing a whole variety of human situations. This new book has been specially written for everyone wanting to know how to make use of counselling techniques in the workplace. It discusses what is counselling, the role of the counsellor, communication skills, body language/verbal behaviour, styles of counselling, managing counselling interviews, and the uses of counselling. The book is complete with helpful checklists, case studies, self-assessment material and points for discussion, key addresses, glossary and index.

160pp illus. 1 85703 093 1.

How to Manage a Sales Team
John Humphries

However good an organisation's product or services, it still has to communicate those benefits to potential customers. The quality of a sales team can be crucial to the success or otherwise of an organisation, especially in the fiercely competitive marketplace of the 1990s. Written by a highly experienced training professional, this book meets the need for a practical handbook for every manager responsible for building or leading a sales team. With its useful checklists and case studies, it covers the whole subject from initial planning to recruitment, sales training, motivation and supervision, controlling budgets and forecasts, running sales meetings, and managing the sales function successfully within the organisation as a whole. John Humphries BSc has 18 years' professional experience as a management trainer.

160pp, 1 85703 079 6.

How to Manage an Office
Ann Dobson

Good office management is one of the keys to success in any organisation. The benefits are a happy and productive staff, satisfied customers, and a sound base from which to tackle such issues as growth and change within the organisation. Written by an experienced office manager and business consultant, this book suggests a complete practical framework for the well run office. It discusses what an office is for, the office as communications, the office as workplace, equipment, hygiene, health and security, external appearances, managing visitors, handling orders and information, managing office supplies, the office budget, staff management, and managing an office move.

160pp illus. 1 85703 049 4.

How to Manage People at Work
John Humphries

'These days, if a textbook on people management is to succeed, it must be highly informative, reliable, comprehensive – and eminently user-friendly. Without doubt, *How to Manage People at Work* is one such book. Written in an attractive style that should appeal to any first-line manager who has neither the time nor the energy to cope with heavy reading, John Humphries has tacked his extremely wide subject ably and well. Rightly or wrongly, it has always been my experience that one has only to read the first couple of pages of any textbook on people management to discover whether or not the author enjoys an empathy with the people at the sharp end – and here is one author who, for my money, has passed the test with flying colours.' *Progress/NEBS Management Association.*

160pp illus. 1 85703 068 0. Second edition.

How to Employ & Manage Staff
Wendy Wyatt

This easy to use handbook is intended for all young managers, supervisors and students whose work will involve them in recruiting and managing staff. Ideal for quick reference, it provides a ready-made framework of modern employment practice from recruitment onwards. It provides a clear account of how to apply the health & safety at work regulations, how to handle record-keeping, staff development, grievance and disciplinary procedures, maternity and sick leave and similar matters for the benefit of the organisation and its employees. The book includes a useful summary of current employment legislation and is complete with a range of model forms, letters, notices and similar documents. Wendy Wyatt GradIPD is a Personnel Management and Employment Consultant; her other books include *Recruiting Success* and *Jobhunt*.

176pp illus. 1 85703 167 9. Second edition.

How to Conduct Staff Appraisals
Nigel Hunt

Managers and organisations neglect staff appraisal at their peril today. But what exactly is staff appraisal? Is it something to be welcomed or feared? Why is it now so vital, and what are the benefits? Should senior as well as junior staff undergo appraisal, and how could this be done? Which managers should do the appraisals, and how should they start? This book, now in a new edition, sets out a basic framework which every manager can use or adapt, whether in business and industry, transport, education, health and public services. It is for the manager who realises how much depends on helping each individual, regardless of position, achieve their real potential at work. Nigel Hunt is a consultant in occupational testing, selection, appraisal, vocational assessment, and management development. He is a Graduate Member of the British Psychological Society, and Associate Member of the Institute of Personnel & Development. 'Informative... Points for discussion and cases studies are prominent throughout... the case studies are highly relevant and good.' *Progress/NEBS Management Association Journal.* 'Not all books live up to their promises. This one does. At the price it is a bargain.' *British Journal of Administrative Management.*

154pp illus. 1 85703 117 2. Second edition.

How to Communicate at Work
Ann Dobson

Things only get done properly at work if everyone communicates effectively – whatever their individual role in the organisation. This very practical step-by-step guide gets to the very basics of good communication – what it is and why we need it, how to speak and listen, how to ask and answer questions, how to take messages and use the telephone; how to liaise, negotiate, persuade, offer advice and accept criticism; how to stand up for yourself, dealing with shyness, a difficult boss or angry customer; how to use and understand body language properly, how to cope with visitors, how to store and present information, how to use the English language correctly – and a great deal more, illustrated throughout with examples and case studies. Written by an experienced office staff trainer this book will be a real help to all young people starting a new job, or older individuals returning to work after time away.

192pp illus. 1 85703 103 2.